THE
STAIRWAY

BRIAN SIMMONS

THE
STAIRWAY

BRIAN
SIMMONS

THE STAIRWAY

The Stairway by Brian Simmons
Published by Stairway Ministries
129 Bull Hill Lane
West Haven CT 06516
203-934-0880

Unless otherwise noted all scripture quotations are taken from the New International Version of the Bible. Copyright © 1973, 1978, 1984 by International Bible Society. Used by permission of Zondervan Publishing House. Scripture quotations marked NAS are taken from the New American Standard Bible. Copyright © 1960, 1962, 1963, 1968, 1971, 1972, 1973, 1975, 1977, 1995 by the Lockman Foundation. Used by permission.

ISBN 0-9753464-0-7
Printed in the United States of America

CONTENTS

ACKNOWLEDGEMENTS

Teamwork. The only ones I know that do not like that word are renegades. For those of us who love to work on a team indulge me this opportunity to thank some good people for what they have done.

I want to thank my personal assistant Jennifer Davis. A hero indeed. You have a great gift of making me look good. Jenn, Candice and I hold you as our spiritual daughter. Also, one man that has captured the spirit of creativity like no other, my friend — Ed Tuttle. His gift of art design will be seen by millions in years to come.

To the staff of Gateway Christian Fellowship — you are my team, my friends. I could never say enough about your devotion and sacrifice of love. And the cheerful congregation of Gateway — you make my life a dream fulfilled just to be your pastor and coach.

To my family — God has given you as a gift of love to me. Candice, my one true love. Our daughters Charity and Joy — the delight of my heart is to be your dad. David, my son, a gift from heaven and an answer to my prayer.

Grandchildren — ah, life's secret treasure! Aidan, Rachel, David, Brianna ... and James! My love for you endures forever. Can we do Disneyworld sometime soon?

To my Beloved King, I bow in reverence before Your Stairway and ask: Can I be close to **You**? Draw me, and I will run.

INTRODUCTION

Nail pierced hands molded a man out of the earth. With longing The Image Maker came down and breathed life into man and saw that it was good. With destiny the Holy One spoke with Abram and called him out of the land of his fathers and into the land of promise. And with more purpose than we can comprehend He is calling us up The Stairway into the eternal way of life.

The book of Genesis is a blueprint for the rest of the Bible. The heart of God is laid bare from the beginning for those who have a heart to see it. It was from before the creation of time that He desired us. It is through the spirit of revelation, truly the spirit of discovery that we are able look beyond the miraculous stories of Abraham, Isaac and Jacob and see multifaceted plans of God. We are able see that God's desire from the beginning was to fill the earth with worshippers — to fill the earth with people who He could love and would love him in return. He longed for a creation who would love Him by choice.

God sent a Stairway to Jacob in Genesis 28 and in Christ God has sent a Stairway to us. Jacob was at the end of himself when he had the vision of the stairway. The Lord showed Jacob His divine perspective on his earthly situation. It was then that Jacob chose to not see his circumstances as they were before he laid his head on the stone, but as God saw them.

The lives of Abraham, Isaac and Jacob are filled with choices as it is with us. Jesus Christ is the ladder that reaches from earth to heaven that stretches the gap that our sin has created. It is our most important choice to believe. It is the choice to believe that there is more to wandering through life. It is choosing to believe that we have a high calling to be priests and kings, to be worshippers of the Most Holy God. It is the belief that our ways are not God's ways, and that what we see with our natural eyes is not the heavenly perspective we are called to perceive through. It is the choice to trust and have faith in a God who was, will and always will be. It is walking in love with a God who will go to the ends of the earth to reveal himself to us. If fact He created the earth to love us. It is the choice to believe that Jesus is our only Stairway, and that with every choice we must choose Him.

Chapter One

THE JOURNEY BEGINS!
"LEAVE YOUR COUNTRY...
GO TO THE LAND I WILL SHOW YOU."

The thoughts of God are not the thoughts of man. According to the genealogy of Matthew, the gospel begins with Abraham. *"A record of the genealogy of Jesus Christ the son of David, the son of Abraham"* (Matt.1:1). The promises of God given in this chapter to Abraham are the promises of the gospel — ***"The Scripture foresaw that God would justify the Gentiles by faith, and announced the gospel in advance to Abraham..."*** (Gal.3:8). The first preaching of the gospel is not in Matthew but in Genesis 12. Christ came into the world *"to show mercy to our fathers and to remember His holy covenant, the oath He swore to our father Abraham (Luke 1:72–73)."*

As the men of Babel sought to build for themselves an earthly city, Abram proved his willingness to abandon all in search of a heavenly city. Abraham's entire life is a story of leaving all to follow the Lord. Much like Peter who left his nets and boats and fishing business — so Abram left his country, his family. He continually released everything to God. The gospel of Jesus Christ truly begins with a man named Abram who listened and obeyed God. All of human history has been changed because Abram heard and followed a heavenly vision.

Here is a chapter-by-chapter analysis of the life of Abraham in Genesis:

11 — Abram visited by God, called out of Ur.

12 — Promise of blessing as Abram journeys forth.

13 — Abram separates from his nephew, Lot.

14 — Abram the conqueror, tithed 10%, blessed by Melchizedek.

15 — God appears to Abram, and enters into covenant.

16 — Abram produces Ishmael, learns to trust in Yahweh.

17 — God gives the promise of Isaac & sign of circumcision.

18 — Abraham intercedes for Lot.

19 — Lot escapes Sodom, God judges the city.

20 — Abraham recognized as a prophet by Abimelech.

21 — Abraham sees the son of promise born — Isaac.

22 — Abraham offers Isaac as a sacrifice to God.

23 — The death and burial of Sarah.

24 — Abraham's servant seeks a bride for Isaac.

25 — Abraham dies, leaving everything to Isaac.

"The God of Glory" first appeared to Abram while in Ur (Acts 7:2) in a way that Abram could never forget; the God of Glory manifested Himself. The celestial vision resulted in a call to Abram that shaped his destiny. He never dreamed of being called by God.

One day, while he was worshipping other gods in the land of Chaldees, the God of Glory appeared to Him. This "appearing" was so life changing, it enabled him to come out of his pagan, darkened background and accept God's calling on his life. The glory of another world drew Abram out of Ur and to city of God.

This is the first time God "appeared" since He walked with Adam and Eve in the cool of the day. We do not read that He appeared to Abel, or Noah, but to Abram. As a man would speak face to face with his friend, God appears. He saw the **God of Glory!** Perhaps it was this vision that kept Abram moving through his tent-dwelling days. Abram was able to believe God because he was a man of spiritual vision. His future was as real as his present.

Isaac could be offered as a sacrifice because Abram could see ahead to the ultimate sacrifice of Jesus (John 8:56). Abraham, the prophet had seen the crucifixion and resurrection of Jesus prophetically, and knew that his son would be a picture of the coming Messiah. Abram was a man captured with the eternal.

Abram was not told to stay and reform the culture or run for political office. He was called to separate himself and go out of Ur toward another city. He didn't know where he was going, but he did know what he was looking for (Heb.11:10). He was told to leave his country, his kindred, his father's house, and leave for a country that God would lead him to. **"Go to the land *I* will show you."**

Led by revelation, God guides Abram by a vision of the Promised Land. As Abram ventured forth in obedience, further revelation would be given him. If we live up to the light God gives us, He will give us even more. He left all to follow this call. Throughout history God calls His servants to leave all and follow Him. Have you left *all* for Jesus? Abram did not know where he was going, but **He Knew God Was Enough**. This is the path of faith.

The reproach of Abram was in proceeding with God's call when it looked foolish. God is pleased to hide from us all the details of our destiny — he wants our obedient faith. This way of faith looks perilous to others, but it is pleasurable to God. Faith pleases Him. As we step out in obedience we learn lessons and enjoy privileges in our relationship with God that others could only hope for.

GOD'S PROMISES TO ABRAM (12:1–3)

1 *"I will make you into a great nation."*
This new beginning for Abram would bring a blessing. This is a prophecy of the nation of Israel being formed from Abram's lineage. God's blessing would be upon this nation and it will be great before God. Because he had left his nation, God would make Abraham into a great nation. This is incredible, for Sarai had long been barren.

2 *"I will bless you."*
This would more than make up for any loss of leaving his comfort zone. His greatest treasure was this blessing from God! The Father's blessing! Obedience brings the blessing of God. Abram and God were to be friends. Implied in this blessing is fertility, offspring! This blessing would involve an heir, spiritual enjoyment, and material prosperity. He received them all.

God's loving heart is revealed as the One who delights in blessing His people. The idea of blessing is used in Genesis more that any other book: 88 times compared to a total of 310 times in the rest of the Old Testament. God's plan is to bless the world — even you!

3 *"I will make your name great."*[1]
There is one Name that is greater than all (Phil. 2:9–11, Rev.15:4). How would God make Abram's name great? By exalting **His name** in the life of His servant. Every advance Abram made into greatness involved an altar where a fragment of his self-life was offered to God. The Babel-builders sought to make a name for *themselves*, but here we find God saying to Abram, "I will make your name great."

The flesh seizes on any opportunity to exalt itself, even in things of God. The disciples of Jesus often competed over who would be the greatest, just as it is today. God is not against greatness, as long as it originates in Him. Abram had much to go through before God could make his name great.

4 *"You will be a blessing."*
Abram's life from this day forward would bring untold blessing to others. Faith always blesses others. Abram could never have become Abraham if he had not left all to obey the call of God. He became a blessing to the nations because he walked in faith. It is God's desire to make every true believer a blessing to the nations....

5 *"I will bless those who bless you."*
Those who endorsed and affirmed Abram would find enrichment and blessing from God. Those befriending him would receive blessing from the God of Glory.

6 *"Whoever curses you I will curse."*
Anyone who treated Abram with contempt would be dishonored, cursed by God. So great was the blessing of Jehovah upon his life! Those who treated him with disrespect, God would remove blessing from them. This threat upon his enemies would be a source of strength to him all his days of pilgrimage.

7 *"All peoples on earth will be blessed through you."*
Abram was to be a source of blessing to the whole world. No one would find Divine blessing apart from his seed. Salvation would come to the nations through the **seed** of Abraham, Jesus Christ our Lord (Matt.1:1). God's blessing to Abram is only fulfilled as it reached to all the nations of the earth. This is the foundation of world missions. God's plan is not merely for a man, or for a nation,

but for the whole world (John 3:16). Jesus Christ is the Greatest Blessing of the world (Acts 4:12)!

"The Scripture foresaw that God would justify the Gentiles by faith, and announced the gospel in advance to Abraham: "All nations will be blessed through you." So those who have faith are blessed along with Abraham, the man of faith." Galatians 3:8–9

ABRAM ARRIVES IN CANAAN (12:4–9)

"So Abram left, as the Lord had told him; and Lot went with him." Abram was now 75 years old. His father had died. The delay was over. He was told to leave all behind. Instead, he took Lot, his nephew, and others who accompanied them who had converted to the God of Abram. Later, Lot would prove to be a weight upon Abram's soul. When we are called to leave it all and go into the undiscovered country, whatever we choose to take with us will prove to be too heavy to bear.

They went forth from Haran to go into the land of Canaan. With a fresh revelation in his heart, Abram and Sarai ventured forth. Arriving at **Shechem**[2] they camped at the great tree of **Moreh**.[3] It was here that the Lord again appears to Abram. He found the Canaanite in the land, but he also found the Lord. God promised to him that his offspring would inherit the land.

"The Lord appeared to Abram and said, 'To your offspring I will give this land.' So he built an altar there to the Lord." Each time God appeared to Abraham he built an altar. This altar was not for a sin offering but for a burnt offering. A sin offering is for redemption, while a burnt offering is an offering of ourselves to God.

The altar here does not refer to the Lord Jesus' crucifixion and death for us; it refers to the consecration of ourselves to God. It was the kind of altar spoken of in Romans 12:1. The mercy of God caused the Lord Jesus to die for us. The mercy of God provided the cross on which we died with Him and on which the devil was dealt with. By the mercy of God we have His life within, and by His mercy, He will bring us into glory.

God wants everything whole; He does not want a half offering. He cannot accept anything less than absolute and complete consecration.

For what purpose was the burnt offering placed on the altar? It was to be wholly burned. Many of us think that we offer ourselves to God to do this or that for Him, whereas what He wants of us is a burning. He does not need a bullock to plow the field for Him; He wants the bullock to be burned on the altar. God is not after our work, but ourselves. He wants us to offer ourselves to Him and be burned for Him.

The altar does not signify doing something for God but living for God. The altar does not mean having busy activities but having a living for God. No activity or work can replace the altar. The altar is a life that is totally for God. Unlike the sacrifice of the Old Testament, which was utterly burned in one act, the sacrifice of the New Testament, as depicted in Romans 12, is the presenting of our bodies as a living sacrifice. Daily we are consumed on the altar, yet daily we are living; we are ever living, yet ever consumed. This is the sacrifice of the New Testament.

This altar would acknowledge Abram's thankfulness to God for His promise and a commitment to love, serve, and worship Him. When God comes to us, an altar of worship becomes the true response of love to Him. The *altar* shows we are on earth only for God. He is our life, so we put everything on the altar. The Babel-builders made a tower and a name for themselves; Abraham makes an altar and calls on the Name of the Lord. God promised that He would make Abram's name great; here we see Abram making God's Name great....

Wherever Abram had a *tent*, he had an *altar*. The tent-life of separation is sure to produce an altar of heavenly fellowship. An altar means we keep nothing for ourselves — all is given to God. While Abram lived in a tent without foundations, he was looking and waiting for a city with foundations (Heb.11:10). Likewise, we are living in the 'tent'[4] of church life, today waiting for its ultimate consummation — the New Jerusalem, the City of God with foundations

As Abram dwelt in the tent, he lived in the shadow of the New Jerusalem, the Eternal Tabernacle. Abram's tent was the seed that grew into the Tabernacle of the Congregation (Exodus) with its harvest being the New Jerusalem. Even though Abram was promised the land, he was looking for the eternal City. Someday Abraham will say to the Lord, 'I remember the day you came to my tent, now I have come to Your Tent.'

Abram must not look at the Canaanites dwelling in the land, but the promise of God. Instead of being occupied with Satan's power to keep us out of the inheritance, we are called to trust Christ's power to bring us in. Instead of indulging in a spirit of fear, Abram walks in a spirit of worship. He could enjoy the promise of God, and that was enough. This faith led him to build the altar of praise to the Promise Keeper.

The Bible nowhere promises us that our circumstances will always be pleasing and comfortable. Ours is the peace of God, not the peace of circumstances. We are never to judge the rightness of our path by the presence of trials. The path of obedience will always be a test to our flesh. Abram built his altar while surrounded by his enemies. Paul was called to Philippi by a supernatural vision, yet the first thing he encountered was a prison cell.

"From there he went on toward the hills east of Bethel and pitched his tent, with Bethel on the west and Ai on the east. There he built an altar to the Lord and called on the name of the Lord."

How significant this is! Bethel means 'the house of God' and Ai means 'a heap of ruins.' In between these two places Abram pitched his tent. This is clearly a time of decision for Abram. He must turn his back on one or the other. As he journeyed toward the promise, the House of God was before and a heap of ruins behind.

The House of God is drawing us in. We must turn our back forever on the old creation life, which is nothing more than a heap of ruins! Bethel is a house; Ai is a heap. God is bringing His people into the revelation of the House of God. When we call on the Name of the Lord we are showing our utter helplessness. Worship is to walk a lifestyle of dependence upon the Lord, not just sounds coming from our mouths. Abram built an altar of worship and called out to the strength that comes from the Name of the Lord.

ABRAM'S FAILURE IN EGYPT (12:10–20)

Faith will always be tested. This famine was sent as a trial to Abram's faith. So often when we set out to our Promised Land we encounter a famine. You can be right where God wants you to be, and still be faced with severe trials. It is better to suffer in God's path than to be at ease in Satan's. This was a test to see if Abram would stay in the land. Abram journeyed all the way from Chaldea to Canaan on the bare word of the Lord. Would he trust Him now in the time of need or turn to Egypt (Hab. 3:17–18)? Egypt is a figurative picture of alliance with the world.

To go down into Egypt is to depend on the arm of flesh. *"Woe to those who go down to Egypt for help, but do no look to the Holy One of Israel or seek help from the Lord"* (Is. 31:1). There is no mention of Abram building an altar in Egypt. One compromise led to another. While in the far country, Abram lies about his wife, protecting himself by claiming she is his sister. He had more confidence in this scheme than in God's grace.

Abram's sin was a poor example to his wife, to those who accompanied him, and to Pharaoh. He presumed the Egyptians would rather be guilty of adultery than of murder. He cared only for himself and did not trust God to protect him. The fear of man brought a snare to his soul. His fears were hypothetical and his ethics situational. Although known for his faith, Abram fell through unbelief — after God had appeared to him twice! In the description of Abraham in Hebrews 11, this fall is left out. Grace only mentioned his faith!

Sarah must have been a beautiful woman. Remarkable, since she was nearly 65 years old! Pharaoh was advised by others to take beautiful Sarai as a concubine. To do this, in the culture of that day, she must be purchased. To gain his consent, Pharaoh gave Abram sheep, cattle, donkeys, camels, and servants. The wealth of the sinners was laid up for the just.[5] Even in his compromise, God blessed Abram. Our faith fails, but God does not....

Somehow, perhaps by a dream, God showed Pharaoh his sin. He rebuked Abram for lying about his wife; and he sent Abram away in peace. Enriched with the spoils of Egypt, Abram returns to the Promised Land. More than just a lesson on honesty, God was preventing Abram and Sarai from deserting His promise of a chosen nation springing forth. Their offspring would be holy, not perverted by Sarai becoming part of Pharaoh's harem! This is an account of God protecting the future of the covenant.

In Egypt there was no tent, no altar, no calling on the name of the Lord. Abram's time in Egypt was wasted time. It was a detour from the purpose of God. It led to compromise and sin. During their stay in Egypt, Sarai took unto her the maid, **Hagar** (Gen. 16:3). The strife, the jealousy, the trouble that Hagar introduced into Abram's household is well known. If they had not gone to Egypt they would not have taken Hagar. If they had not taken Hagar, there would have been no Ishmael. Beware of going down to Egypt when you are tested. Learn to trust and not be moved when the famine is all around you.

[1] Abraham means 'father of many.' Sarai means 'domineering one.' After God's dealing with her heart, she was changed to Sarah ('noble woman,' or 'princess'). Truly, God made Abram's name great.

[2] Shechem means *'shoulder,'* the place of strength. Shechem was the place where years later our Lord Jesus sat at the well of Jacob weary in His journey.

[3] The great tree of Moreh was where God taught Abram to walk in faith not by sight. Moreh means *'instruction.'* True spiritual knowledge comes from the strength of Christ. God will lead us to a place of true strength and instruct our heart to trust in Him alone.

[4] Paul, the Abraham of the New Testament, was a tent-maker.

[5] This was a foreshadowing of the Exodus from Egypt that would take place centuries later.

Chapter Two

ABRAM HAD A LOT TO LOSE!
"ABRAM HAD BECOME VERY WEALTHY."

Abram starts over. He retraces his steps until once again he finds the place of blessing, where his tent once had been. It was at Bethel that Abram decided to leave the place of anointing and go down to Egypt. Now he returns with humility of heart to rebuild his altar of devotion. Many times we must return to our first love and reexamine our commitment to follow the Lamb. Abram had an altar to return to, as a place where fellowship could be restored. A place where the pilgrim character of a worshipper under the tent. Abram knew where to find God again.

It was at the altar that Abram called on the Name of the Lord. God restored Abram to the place of sweet communion and fellowship once again (Ps.23:3). His faith was not in a plan, but in a Person. His destiny did not mean more to him than His desire to belong to Yahweh.

The grace of God shines brightly even in Abram's trip to Egypt. He returns not only with a broken heart but also with the wealth and spoils of the land. Blessed with possessions Abram became very wealthy (Literal Heb. 'heavy').

Lot, Abram's nephew also amassed livestock, servants, and possessions. It seems even those who 'hung out' with Abram were blessed. Lot lived off Abram's blessing. It is not enough to follow in the tracks of someone who is blessed — we must discover our own track of blessing and fruitfulness in God. Nothing will endure unless it is of God. Our 'borrowed' blessings will fail if we ourselves do not have a link with the Living God.

Lot was an echo, not an example. He saw the faith of Abram but could not hear the voice of God for himself. He was along for the ride. Nothing can be more worthless than an imitation. Are you walking under a Divine influence or a human influence? The blessing of someone else cannot prop us up. The call of God had not reached Lot's heart. He left Ur with Abram, but fell in the plains of Sodom. His personal inheritance had not filled his vision.

"But the land could not support them while they stayed together, for their possessions were so great that they were not able to stay together. And quarreling arose between Abram's herdsmen and the herdsmen of Lot." What was the cause of his fall? The strife between his herdsmen and Abram's? The real cause of Lot's backsliding was his failure to cultivate friendship with God. The strife of the herdsmen did not create the worldliness in Lot. It only manifested it.

The Hebrew word for **Lot** is *'covert, secret, or concealed.'* Everything about Lot was hidden away in his heart. Compromise was a way of life for him. The secret tug of the world drew him away from the place of blessing. He had never really left Ur; he was still an idolater at heart. He looked for the closest thing that resembled Egypt when he chose the rich plains. He chose what would please him without considering the consequences. Lot's possessions were eventually burned in fires of judgment and he ended up living in a cave.

Abram's words displayed the *"meekness of wisdom"* (Jas . 3:13). Lot would have had nothing if it had not been for Abram. He could have told Lot to leave. He willingly deferred to his nephew for the sake of keeping peace. He loved God and hated strife. It was not compromise. It was wisdom. They were relatives. They had a vast inheritance they could share together. But instead of sharing, they quarreled.

"The Canaanites and Perizzites were also living in the land at that time. So Abram said to Lot, 'Let's not have any quarreling between you and me, or between your herdsmen and mine, for we are brothers." Why quarrel in the presence of the Canaanites and Perizzites? Why would brethren contend with one another before the lost of this world? Cannot the God of heaven give them wisdom to settle their difficulty without a humiliating argument before the unbelievers?

Abram looked at things from God's viewpoint. This is why he could choose the path of peace over the path of personal rights. Abram took what was left. He turned from strife, refusing to war with his brethren. The way of peace is a pleasant way, although it may cost us in the short term. This is the way of faith. God promised him the land, he could let it go and wait for His perfect timing. Abram surrendered control and let God be his inheritance.

God will always treat you better than men when we leave the choice up to Him! You will be satisfied with the portion **God** chooses for you (Ps.16:5–6, 84:11). What security faith brings to the heart! Trust in God is resting in His goodness. Abram would later be given **All** of the land as his inheritance as a Friend of God. Abram is a picture of the man of the Spirit:

➤ He walked in wisdom.

➤ He had love for his brother without prejudice.

➤ He valued unity.

➤ He was concerned about his witness to the heathen.

➤ He gave up his own rights and desires for wealth.

➤ He chose a tent and enjoyed fellowship with God.

Abram was quite generous. Lot, in his greed, took full advantage of it. The flesh of man is opportunistic. We are graspers by nature. To yield, to defer to others, is a work of the Spirit of God within us. With the eye of an appraiser Lot looked over the land and chose Sodom, the place destined for judgment. Lot chose the world. He walked by sight, what looked good to the eyes (I John 2:15–17). Lot was led astray; leaving the place of blessing to go into the place of judgment.

Lot became an official of Sodom seated at its gate (Gen.19:1). What did he gain by separating from Abram? Nothing at all. He became polluted by the men of Sodom. Instead of bringing light into Sodom, darkness entered his soul (II Pet.2:7–8). Lot is a picture of a believer who lives far below his calling and destiny. He preferred the well-watered plains to Abram's altar. By wrong choices and subtle compromises, we bring many sorrows into our lives. Beware of seeking to make the best of both worlds. Seek first His Kingdom!

When Abram offered the choice to Lot, he should have said, 'Uncle, I choose you. God is with you. My choice is your choice.' Every young person likes to be separated from the older generation. Lot missed the will of God by separating from the called one, Abram. There is protection, covering, and anointing when we walk with those who walk with God. Our flesh would rather 'do it on our own' but God's way is to walk in fellowship with called ones.

It was God's purpose to separate Abram from his land of birth, from his kinsmen, from every earthly attachment. In the separation of Abram and Lot, God's purpose is finally realized. Abram had a *Lot* to lose. Now Abram is left alone with God.

GOD'S PROMISE TO FAITHFUL ABRAM (13:14–18)

Alone with God, Abram receives another Divine visitation. God tells Abram to lift up his eyes and look at his inheritance. Lot lifted up his physical eyes (v.10); Abram lifted up his spiritual eyes — knowing it was better to wait than to strive. Abram waited for God to give it, Lot took it for himself.

This is a new Abram coming forth … His personal self-interest is put behind him. We see no desire to preserve his pride or position. He uses spiritual authority to bless and to give, as personal rights take the 'back seat' to his testimony before the Canaanites. God has worked deeply in his heart.

God tied together the promise of the land and the promise of the offspring. God compares the vast number of his future offspring to the dust of the earth. It would be his offspring that ultimately inherits the land of promise — even the land chosen by Lot.

As Abram walked through the land he would see the vast extent of the promises of God. The One who prepared the Holy Land will prepare the Holy Seed.

Abram moved his tents. In anticipation of more from God, he ventured forth in faith. He was willing to be a pilgrim that always had to 'move his tents' when fresh revelation came. The pain of strife and separation gave way to a fresh revelation of the promise. Notice the progression of verse eighteen:

"So Abram moved his tents and went to live near the great trees of Mamre at Hebron, where he built an altar to the *Lord*." Here are the 4 realities of the Abraham journey:

Obedience — "Abram moved his tent."

Anointing — "Mamre" = 'fatness', place of the anointing.

Fellowship — "Hebron" = 'fellowship or communion.'

Worship — Abram "built an altar to the Lord."

The chapter ends as it began — Abram building an altar to the Lord at the place of the anointing. Lot chose Sodom, Abram chose the Lord! From the beginning of his history Abram was a man of devotion to God. As a worshipper, he could respond correctly to strife and wait patiently for the Lord to fulfill His promise. In faith, Abram was a man far ahead of his time. He is an example to all his "spiritual seed." Abram's walk is deepening. He was entering into sweet fellowship with his Friend. He has learned that God is faithful … now he is ready for battle.

THE TRUE WORLD WAR I (14:1–16)

This chapter opens with the first war mentioned in Scripture. Four kings went to war against five kings. These kings were ruling over powerful city-states. The territory they fought over was the land bridge through which the commerce of Egypt and the four eastern states must pass. Whoever controlled this land bridge would have a monopoly on international trade. As the battle raged, Lot was taken captive … He had laid up treasures on earth only to have thieves break through and steal. One of Lot's servants escaped and brought to Abram the news of his nephew's captivity.

Abram did not respond with, 'Well, that is what happens when you make the wrong choice. I'll just let him suffer — God may be teaching him a lesson!' **No**, Abram, the Friend of God had no root of bitterness. He moved with compassion. With 318 trained servants, Abram took off to rescue the captives. So must we. When we hear that a brother is overtaken in a fault, our first response must be to restore and heal — not condemn and ignore (Gal. 6:1). Boldness filled Abram's heart (Prov. 28:1). He went into battle for his brother. Showing no hesitancy, he pursued the conquerors. He brought back Lot, his servants, and all the goods that were stolen. Unlike Cain, Abram became his brother's keeper.

The five kings should have been victorious against the four. But the four kings defeated the five, taking Sodom captive. What happened in the natural with Lot and his family was a picture of what happened in his spirit — he was held captive by the spirit of this world! Abram entered spiritual warfare from a place of fellowship (Hebron). The four kings were of Mesopotamia while the five kings were of the Jordan Valley. Here are the names of the kings:

For

Amraphel: 'keeper of gods, speaker of mysteries'
King of Babylon: 'confusion, mixture' i.e. *worldly*
Arioch: 'great one, lion like'
King of Ellasar:[6] 'revolting from God' i.e. *rebellion*
Kedorlaomer: 'handful or bundle of sheaves' (control)
King of Elam:[7] ' secret' i.e. *false religion*
Tidal: 'renown, fearsome, high knowledge'
King of Goiim: 'peoples' i.e. *intimidation*

Against

Bera: 'son of thought, declaring'
King of Sodom: 'their secret' i.e. *unrighteousness*
Birsha: 'son of wickedness'
King of Gomorrah: 'ruined heap' i.e. *shameful ways*
Shinab: 'sharpened desire' or father of changing'
King of Admah: 'dirt' i.e. *clever deceit*
Shemeber: 'superior brilliance, name of force'
King of Zeboiim: 'pompous ones' i.e. *arrogant pride*
King of **Bela:** (Zoar) 'swallow up, devour'

The four kings, led by Kedorlaomer, held five kings in servitude for 12 years. During the 13th year they began to revolt.[8] In the 14th year of their bondage, King Kedorlaomer and his allies went on a rampage to punish the rebels. They smote and conquered the giants of Canaan. This makes Abram's victory over Kedorlaomer and his partners even more significant. Abram defeated those who prevailed over the giants!

These kings in the land were representative of the spiritual powers keeping Abram from his inheritance; dark powers sent to rob him of his destiny. Abram learned the principles of spiritual warfare and fought for the blessings of others; thus becoming a picture of a true intercessor. God sent confusion among these regional powers. They fought against each other until they ended up in the tar pits ('slime pits') in the valley of Siddim ('wild country'). Here are their giants:

Rephaites: 'giants'
    Ashteroth Karnaim: 'double-horned' or 'fearful ones'
Zuzites: 'prominent ones, wild beasts'
    Ham: 'darkened'
Emites: 'terrible ones, terrorists'
    Shaveh Kiriathaim: 'double-cities'
Horites: 'cave dwellers, angry ones'
    Seir: 'rough country' or 'where demons dwelt'

Abram is here called the Hebrew ('one who crossed over'). The patriarch takes his own personal army (318 disciples), trained in his own house (local church) and won a great victory. What a bold step of faith to take only 318 men against the kings and their expert armies of war! Abram moves under Divine favor knowing that God is with him.

This is a picture of how we must act in faith when we see a brother trapped in sin. We must rise up and do battle for them. Abram's burden was to get his nephew back. He chased them to a place called Hobah ('hiding place') where he took back what was stolen. Overcomers are those who recover all the enemy has taken. We must go into every hiding place of darkness until all is restored.

Abram, the man of faith, conquered the kings of the land. He was victorious. He truly crossed over into his inheritance by faith. In doing so, many were rescued. What was the secret of Abram's victory? Could it be that someone was interceding for him behind the scenes? One who had authority with God ... an intercessor ... a priest?

We need to slaughter some kings daily! The kings in our mind, the kings in our emotions and will. After we have finished our slaughter of the kings, our Melchizedek will come to meet with us — celebrating our victory. Our victory always makes Christ manifest. Today, Christ, our Melchizedek is interceding in heaven for all the overcoming ones. While He intercedes, we slaughter the kings of a fallen planet.

MELCHIZEDEK, PRIEST OF GOD MOST HIGH (14:17–24)

As Abram returns from battle, two kings meet him — the King of Sodom offering the spoils of war, and the King of Salem[9] (Melchizedek) bringing bread and wine. This is all deeply significant and affects Abram powerfully for the rest of his life![10] Overwhelmed with the revelation of who God is and the victory God won for him, Abram abandons all to the Lord.

After great victories expect to face new temptations. This was both *a temptation* to Abram to take things — and *a revelation* of **"God Most High."** Melchizedek comes to Abram while the king of Sodom wants to reward Abram. What a picture! The king of Sodom is willing to give Abram all he wants of the goods of this world. This would mean considerable wealth for Abram. Yet, here comes the King of Salem, ready to bless Abram in the Name of **El Elyon, God Most High!**

The goods of Sodom may make life comfortable, but the **"bread and wine"** will refresh his spirit. The royal priest, Melchizedek presents to Abram the blessing of "El Elyon," **God Most High**, Creator of heaven and earth, the God of **Fullness** within the veil. Abram is blessed in **This** new Name (revelation). All this happened in the **"King's Valley,"** the low place where we meet the **King**!

---

⁶ Ellasar was an ancient region of Asia.

⁷ Elam is the ancient name of Persia, present day Iran.

⁸ The first mention of 13 in the Bible (the number of rebellion).

⁹ Salem later became the city of Jeru*salem*.

¹⁰ In John 8:56 Jesus said that "Abraham rejoiced at the thought of seeing my day; he saw it and was glad." Abraham saw the day of Jesus as Melchizedek came out to meet him with bread and wine, the elements of Holy Communion.

Chapter Three

MELCHIZEDEK
"PRIEST OF GOD MOST HIGH"

Melchizedek did not appear because Abram sinned, but because Abram gained a victory over kings. He came to nourish the victor with bread and wine. Who was Melchizedek, this Priest — King of Salem who prophesied blessing to Abram? Hebrew tradition states he was **Shem**, survivor of the flood and the oldest living man.

Most Bible students believe that Melchizedek was a 'Christophany' or a preincarnation appearance of the Lord Jesus Christ. Jesus is our Priest and our King. Salem means 'peace.' Jesus is **the King of Peace!** He came from a "Salem" not on earth, but from a heavenly realm (Gal. 4:26). Jesus is our Melchizedek (Ps.110:4, Heb.7:23–24). Abram had a face-to-face encounter with Jesus Christ the Son of God! The Friend of God met the Son of God.

The priesthood of Aaron was always interrupted by death. The sons of Aaron were continually taking the priesthood, only to die and pass the mantle to another. Jesus has died once and for all and He now rules as a High Priest after the order of Melchizedek over both Jew and Gentiles (Heb.7:2). He walks in Royal Authority and He is the King of Righteousness ('Melchizedek').

Melchizedek served communion to Abram and the power of this communion imparted life to them to bear a child! Isn't this just like the Lord Jesus? He comes to us when we are battle weary — on the eve of a great temptation. He not only refreshes our spirit, He prepares us for the next level of conflict. With a fresh glimpse into His heart we are filled with grace to encounter the enemy again. The next time you are tempted, remember the mercies of our Lord Jesus, Possessor of heaven and earth.

This revelation produced a remarkable thing in Abram. He saw God in a new way. He was now the highest over the principalities and powers that fought against Abram in the slime pits! He gave Melchizedek a "tithe" or "tenth" of all the spoils of the battle (Heb.7:4). The King of Sodom stood there and witnessed Abram giving over a tenth of Sodom's wealth to this mysterious priest.

The blessing of El Elyon gave Abram strength to refuse the offer from the king of Sodom. Abram found a higher love. Something was imparted to Abram that made the things of this life seem like trash. Abram saw that the God of heaven and earth loved him … this was all he needed!

The priesthood of Melchizedek was truly unique. No genealogy is given for him. He is without beginning and without ending (Heb.7:3)! Abram did not bless Melchizedek; Melchizedek blessed Abram. This King of Salem steps out of history to reveal El Elyon to victorious Abram. This was the Ancient of Days, the King of the Ages, the I Am. He lives to make continual intercession for us as our Great High Priest after the order of Melchizedek. This Priesthood receives tithes of all (Heb.7:4). In paying of tithes to Melchizedek, Abram acknowledged God's grace in giving him the victory.

Melchizedek was a priest on behalf of whom? Not the Jews, for Abram was yet to have a son. It was on behalf of the Gentiles. God established a priesthood over the *Gentiles* before He brought forth a priesthood over the Jews. Melchizedek was a gentile king over a gentile city. Gentiles are in the heart of God even in Genesis! This gentile king is found with a revelation of God to impart to Abram.

This mysterious gentile priest blesses the father of many nations. As Creator of heaven and earth, God is over the nations, not just Abram and his clan. This Most High God has given an inheritance to all peoples (Deut.32:8, Dan.4:17).

There is no mention that Lot ever thanked Abram after his rescue or built an altar of gratitude to God. Lot was a man of the world; he merely went back to Sodom. But Abram's testimony was, **"I have raised my hand to the Lord, God Most High, Creator of heaven and earth, and have taken an oath that I will accept nothing...."**

This God would now be his Source and Provider. A "blessed" man does not need the world's help — God is enough. Abram went to war in the power of that Name. The power to overcome the world was in his faith in God Most High (I John 5:4). The goods of Sodom were nothing compared to the revelation of God's love for Him. The bread and wine were an invitation from God to feast on Him, not the things of this life. Nothing else attracted his affection.

So, Abram refuses to be enriched by this king of Sodom. How could Abram be a Deliverer if he himself was not delivered? This was the path of separation that was always before Abram. Would God be enough? Could he leave it all behind? May the Lord keep us all true to Him in these days of snares and compromises. What are the lessons we can learn from this chapter?

➤ We see the *result* of the decision Abram made in Chapter 13.
It is a divine commentary on making right choices. Lot chose
Sodom and self-interest and nearly lost it all. Abram chose to
pursue peace and was given grace to win a military victory. Lot
trusted in himself and became enslaved. Abram trusted God
and became respected and honored. Our decisions reveal our
character and point to our destiny.

➤ The *sovereignty of God* is seen in the way God moved the affairs
of men to accomplish His purposes. Even international events
are ordered by One who loves His people. There is another side
to the news!

➤ God works through *men*. Abram was God's instrument of
deliverance for Lot. Melchizedek was God's instrument of
blessing for Abram.

➤ We can never take for ourselves any *glory* for the victories God has
won for us. All the 'spoils' of victory are His. We must be cautious
in touching money and material things that belong to God.

A HEAVENLY VISION (15:1–6)
"Do not be afraid ... I am your very great reward."

Because he rejected the things of Sodom, Abram is granted a
fresh revelation of God as his Shield and Great Reward. It is
better for Abram to be hidden behind *Jehovah's shield* than
to take refuge in the things of the world. Knowing God as his
Reward is infinitely better than whatever Abram lost. God is
our Shield that we might rest in Him, and our Reward that we
might wait on Him. In vision form, God came to Abram and
promised to be His Defender. In tender grace He quieted the
troubled heart of His friend.

Abram looked for city whose Architect and Builder is God.
He declined to take even a shoelace from Sodom. God more than

makes it up to Abram. He is compensated with a new revelation ...
God is his Shield, God is his great Reward.

God wants to fill our future! **He Himself** will be more than a
Rewarder — He is our *very great reward*. Life's greatest treasure
is the knowledge of God. What greater pleasure is there than
intimacy with God as our very great Reward? True rewards are
found in **Him**, not in the favor of others. Others will view us in
light of our weakness — God sees us in light of our destiny. Our
true identity is wrapped up in God as our Understander and as our
Great Reward.

Abram was a wise intercessor. He received this word of favor
and took the opportunity to ask his **"Sovereign Lord"** for a child.
This was a prayer of faith. Abram wanted a son! He had heard
this promise before — but where is the son? He had waited ten
years in the land already. All he had in his household was Eliezer of
Damascus. Why had God taken so long?

We are so prone to mistake delays for denials. God uses delays
to instruct us, break us, and leave us dependent upon **Him Alone**.
We will trust anything but God. He will take everything from us
and leaves us only with a promise ... will we believe the bare word
of the Lord?

Under the prevailing custom of the day, if Abram died childless,
his household servant would become the heir. But what about the
promise of offspring? The inheritance must come to a son, not a
servant. Sonship is the basis of inheritance (Gal.4:6–7). The Word
of the Lord came to him with the promise; **"a son coming from
your own body will be your heir."**

Abram was then given a prophetic sign as Yahweh took him
outside his tent to gaze at the heavens and count the stars. Each
star he saw would represent an heir, a descendant. This prophetic
gesture had a profound effect on Abram. He was speaking to the
One who made the sky. From that moment on, he believed the

Lord, and *"it was credited to him as righteousness."* This encounter with the "Sovereign Lord" forever changed his destiny. He no longer considered the impossibility of having a child. God counted this faith as an equivalent of righteousness. God was pleased with His friend.

Abram believed that God would give him a son. We believe God has already given us His Son, Jesus Christ. Our faith is likewise counted as righteousness. We are heirs of Abram's blessing and all the blessings of Jesus Christ. God sees us as righteous as Jesus Christ!

In Genesis 13:14–17 God uses the **Dust** of the land as a prophetic sign. In Chapter Fifteen the *stars* of the heavens that speak of offspring. The sons of Abraham are both **Natural** (dust) and **Heavenly** (stars). Israel is the nation of descendants from Abraham. The Church (Jew and Gentile) is the spiritual Israel (Gal.3:26–29). The sand on the seashore and the stars of the skies ... both speak of the **Power** of God to raise up sons and daughters that love Him and believe His promise. The **Seed** will be a corporate people on earth.

The faith of Abraham is the faith that is precious to God. It is the kind of faith that believes that God will work in us to bring forth Christ, **The Seed**. It is entirely the work of God, grace through faith, that the promise is fulfilled. All we have is Eliezer and all we can do is Ishmael, and neither of them counts for the fulfillment of God's purpose. It must be God Himself. After we have truly become nothing, God will work Himself into us — which will bring forth Christ as the **Seed** and will bring us into Christ as the **Land**. The day will come when we will live in Him as our land.

This heavenly gaze widened Abram's vision. He began to see the supernatural in a new way. From now on, it would be the power of the *Creator of the stars* that would fulfill the promise. Abram went from limited **Tent** vision into unlimited **Heavenly** vision (Eph.5:14)! This Word from the Lord addressed the two main fears of his life: 1) His fear of position and poverty — God as Shield would be his defender. 2) His fatherhood — God would provide for him an heir, a son! If you turn your gaze to heaven your fears would melt away too!

GOD'S PROPHETIC COVENANT WITH ABRAM (15:7–20)

Abram's faith released a fresh revelation. The Lord reminds him Who redeemed him — and Who guides his life (Isa.29:2). Faithful is the One who called him — and He would be faithful to bring him into the land (I Thess.5:24). Between being **"brought out"** and being **"given the land"** there was a season of growing for Abram. As a pilgrim, he learned to trust in God along the way ... like you and I.

Now this friend of God asks for a sign — **"How can I know...?"** Abram believed, but needed reassurance to treasure in his heart. Even the faithful need help! God will ratify His promise to Abram with a *unique prophetic picture*. God directs Abram to prepare for a sacrifice. Abram asks for a son, God asks for a sacrifice. God still speaks through the sacrifice of His Son as a Sign to the nations that God has loved the world and provided salvation for all.

A heifer, a goat, and a ram — each three years old, along with a dove and a young pigeon were presented to the Lord. Divided in half, the animals were killed. These sacrifices were all 'types' or pictures of the Lord Jesus Christ. They were tame animals — the Lord Jesus Christ was yielded fully to the Father. **"Bring Me"** tells us the sacrifice is not just for man but for God.

The heifer, goat, and ram signify the crucified Christ, for they were cut in half. Jesus was cut, crucified for us. The two birds were kept alive. They signify the resurrection of Christ, the One who now lives to rule in the heavens. Each of these 5 (number of grace) animals are types of Christ.

The young *heifer* speaks of the freshness of His vigor. The *goat* is the animal used in the sin-offering (Lev.4:28, 5:6). The *ram* is the animal of consecration and substitution. Jesus is the **Ram** caught in the thicket on Mt. Moriah (Gen. 22:13). The birds speak of the **One** who came down from heaven and was raised again to return to heaven. The **Two** living birds (dove and pigeon) bear *witness* of Christ as the resurrected One living in us as for us. Two is the number of witness. The "dove" rested on Him as He began His ministry. Jesus walked and taught and healed and blessed the hearts of men for three years; and after the three years He became the sacrifice for sin.

The dividing of these animals speaks of the blood covenant that God presents to humanity. What is described here is the way of covenant, the way one made a covenant with another. By cutting the animals in half (except the birds), it signified that the promise passed between the hearts and organs and inner being of those who made a covenant. It was sealed in blood.

So Abram separated the sacrifices — making a lane or path with the halves of the animals on each side. As he waited throughout the day for God to move, he drove away the buzzards and "unclean" birds of prey (doubts) that came after the carcasses. This pictures the one who receives the promise is required to deal with doubts and conflicting thoughts. Like buzzards circling overhead, the enemy comes to steal the promise — the hope of fulfillment from our heart. We must arise and drive away every fear and lie of the enemy. The longer the wait, the more numerous the doubts. Under the heat of a burning day we can easily grow weary and faint. Be alert to this strategy! See Habakkuk 2:3, Lam. 3:26, Romans 8:25

As the sun sets, a deep sleep came upon him like a **"dreadful darkness."** The heavy veil of night fell. This **"deep sleep"** was a form of Divine ecstasy or trance — much like what happened to Adam (Gen. 2:21). Abram was filled with awe! The Lord now appears in this surreal setting in a prophetic act to confirm His promise to Abram.

What a picture of waiting on God! We believe the promise, only to pass through the darkness of waiting on God. We are left in the "dreadful darkness" of the fulfillment being out of our control. Only God knows when the promise will be realized. The flesh withers, our strength evaporates, doubts clog our way — when will He come through for me? Abram learned through the darkness the principle of **Death** and **Crucifixion**. The inheritance can only be gained through suffering (Heb.5:8–9, Rom.8:17, Acts 14:22, Phil.1:29).

For those with prophetic promises yet to be fulfilled, hear this: Even in your dreadful darkness, deal with your doubts and wait, wait on the Lord! Your Faithful God will not disappoint you.

The dreadful darkness was a picture of what was coming for Abram's offspring. Abram's descendants would become slaves in a strange country and mistreated for 400 years (*1891 B.C. – 1491 B.C.*). Notice that God did not tell Abram that it would be in Egypt. There are times the Lord will withhold from us what we do not need to know. What a strange thing it would be for the generation brought out of Egypt to read this accurate prophecy of the Exodus....

Their deliverance would come in the **"fourth generation;"** the generation of Moses and Aaron. Afterwards, they would return to the land with great possessions (Ex.12:35–36). The righteous God had set a time when the sins of the Amorites (Canaanites) would reach its "full measure." How much more patient is the Lord than you and I!

All of this was confirmed as a smoking fire pot with a blazing torch appeared and passed majestically between the pieces of the sacrifice, consuming them in **Holy Fire** (Judges 6:21, Ex.19:18, II Sam.22:9, Isa.6:4)! It is while Abram sleeps that Father and Son come to him, walking between the pieces of his faith, and confirming the promise! The battle was won while Abram slept.

So is the Everlasting Covenant; planned from eternity, **Cut** on the work of the **Cross** and ratified by the resurrection of our Lord

Jesus. All that is left for us is to **Rest** (put the flesh to sleep) and wait! Jesus walking through the severed pieces of the sacrifice is a statement that when Abram fails to keep the covenant, Jesus will pay the price for him ... and for us.

In every dark trial, the believer has the 'Blazing Torch' of Jesus with us — a Light shining in a dark place (II Pet.1:19). He turns night into day and shines brightly upon our path. Walk in the light of this **Blazing Torch!** The day will come when the blazing torch becomes a bush of fire, then a pillar of fire ... then it will come to rest upon the heads of every disciple (Acts 2).

God's promise to Abram, spoken that mysterious night, becomes the 'title deed' to the land. He is given the boundaries of the expanse of the land of promise. Rivers will be part of the inheritance — and land occupied by the enemy. Powerful princes will someday be dethroned as they march into the fullness of their inheritance. The God that walked between the sacrifices will walk in the Land and conquer their foes (Is. 43:1–7)!

God passing between the pieces of the sacrifice is a picture of Jesus passing through the cross. Abraham learned that the inheritance of the land was based on the death of the cross. Only those who have passed through the cross will see the burning lamp and blazing torch.

The Lord promises, **"To your descendants I will give this land, from the river of Egypt to the great river, the Euphrates — the land of the Kenites, Kenizzites, Kadmonites, Hittites, Perizzites, Rephaites, Amorites, Canaanites, Girgashites, and Jebusites."** These 'ites' were symbolic of spiritual powers that possessed the inheritance given to Abram. They would have to be driven out of the land and conquered for the **Spiritual Seed** to fully inherit the promises of God.

In order for you to take **Your** inheritance you must be prepared to fight the good fight of faith, for God has given you the land (your spiritual inheritance). Every force within your portion you have a right to overcome. For the word of God has spoken and given you the promise of inheritance ... it is yours for the taking!

"Now Sarai, Abram's wife, had borne him no children. But she had an Egyptian maidservant named Hagar; so she said to Abram, "The Lord has kept me from having children. Go, sleep with my maidservant; perhaps I can build a family through her." Genesis 16:1–2

Chapter Four

ISHMAEL
"NOW SARAI... HAD BORNE HIM NO CHILDREN."

Sarai was barren — childless. In her desperation she tries to nudge the arm of God and convince her husband into fathering a child with her servant, Hagar. This was a test for Abram, for he had waited so long for the promised son. In Chapter 15 Abram listens to the voice of God, in Chapter 16 he listens to the voice of Sarai and takes Hagar unto himself. All of this is an example of the wisdom of the flesh, not the wisdom of God. Faith can wait and rest until the promise is fulfilled. The flesh has to 'make it happen' anyway it can.

Notice how many times Abram's faith is tested! First, his faith had to overcome *the ties of nature*, for God's call took him away from his country and his kindred. Shortly after arriving in Canaan, Abram's faith was tested in *severe circumstances* — there was famine in the land. Then he faced a painful trial with respect to *strife with* a *brother,* (his nephew) and the separation it led to. Later, he was still tested over his *courage* and his *love* for Lot who had been captured and needed rescuing. Abram was tested over his *desire for wealth* as the King of Sodom tempted him with the rewards of battle. Now we see the patriarch led by the suggestion of his wife to *take things into his own hands* when God seems to delay.

Look at this pattern again and realize that **You** will be tested in the very same things! Remember: these are the tests that the one favored by God must endure. If you have not yet faced these tests, you will. There are still more trials ahead for the friend of God....

1 *The ties of nature.*
   Is our passion with our loved ones or God?

2 *By severe circumstances.*
   Will we trust God with strong faith?

3 *Strife with a brother.*
   Can we take the lowest place, even loving those who promote themselves?

4 Courage
   Will we fight for the one who messed up his own life?

5 *Desire for wealth?*
   Is integrity that important to faith?

6 *Waiting for God.*
   Will we take things into our own hands?

The Hebrew word for Hagar means *'ensnaring.'* The ways of the flesh ensnare us and lead us into folly. Hagar is an Egyptian and thereby a descendant of Ham (Gen.10:6). From Noah's prophecy we know it is God's plan for the Messiah to come through Shem.

Ishmael was a good idea. The flesh will not wait for the promise; it always has a better idea. Cleverness is not a spiritual gift; it is a stumbling block. When we substitute our wonderful ideas, inventions, programs, and schemes for a simple faith that waits, we end up in confusion and heartache. When we try to fulfill promises or prophecies with our clever strategies we are acting in the flesh. God's work must not only be free from sin, it must be free from self-effort. Nothing we originate can satisfy God's heart. The snares of the enemy can actually be our own ideas that are given birth by impatience.

During God's delays our flesh gets agitated and rash. 'God is not coming through — maybe I could have misunderstood — maybe I need to *do* something?' The delays of God expose our unbelief. It is one thing to believe the promise at first, and quite another thing to hold fast in faith when nothing seems to be happening. Waiting teaches us the ways of God as we **Trust** in the dark.

True faith is **Never** in a hurry. Patience will always be the proof of enduring faith (Heb. 6:12). When we know our Friend we can wait on His timing! In time, the foolishness of our 'ideas' will be seen. Hagar was elated over the honor of bearing a son for Abram. Blaming her husband for the mess, Sarai now became jealous. Her attitude sours toward her servant until Hagar had to flee.

So often, when we see the mistake of acting in the flesh we will punish others with our sorrow and shame. An outburst of wounded pride only makes matters worse. When we are wrong we must humble ourselves and confess it. God will deliver us.

Hagar takes off for Egypt (Shur is on the way towards Egypt). But God stops her with a Divine Encounter. The **"angel of the Lord"** appeared to her in the wilderness. God will often lead us into a wilderness to meet us there (Hos. 2:14, Rom. 5:6).

The 'angel' does not call her Abram's wife, but Sarai's servant. She is commanded to return to Sarai with the promise that she too will have descendants too numerous to count. Good advice: Return, submit, and inherit the promise! She will have to return to Sarai and give birth to her son. God does not speak to Abram or Sarai but to Hagar. Because of Abram's unbelief, God apparently does not speak to Abram for 13 years … Quite a price to pay for doubting the promise of God.

The prophecy is given, complete with the name of her son — and his destiny. His name is to be Ishmael, or *'God hears/understands.'* He will be **"a wild donkey of a man"** whose lifestyle is in hostility to all his brothers. He will be untamed, undisciplined, wild, and warlike. Ishmael speaks of the **Old Nature**, the beast nature, the flesh! He was a 'wild Adam.' This is the word for a wild ass or donkey that is untamed and needs bridled.

By contrast, the **Ox Nature** is the new nature, the nature of our Lord Jesus, meek and serving. The ox will work in a yoke, but the wild donkey never comes under the yoke of another. Ishmael becomes the father of the Arabs, traditional enemies of the Jewish people. Mohammed, the founder of Islam came from the line of Ishmael. Islam is a religion that is extremely difficult to penetrate with the gospel of Christ. What great damage and bondage results in Abram's decision to make it happen (Gal. 4:22–26).

The angel of the Lord found Hagar where God finds all of us — by the well of water in the wilderness. She names this well, "Beer Lahai Roi" which means **"the well of the Living One who sees me!"** She recognized that the angel of the Lord was none other than the Living One who saw her in her distress. This same God sees you today — right where you are. He knows your distress and your tendency to flee when difficulty comes. In your wilderness He is there with fresh revelation of who **He** is. Another translation calls this well, 'the well of Living sight' (revelation)!

This encounter at the "well" reminds us of later time when Jesus would journey to a well just to meet a woman who had a history of running from God. At this well of Sychar the **Living One** again sees into the heart of a woman and speaks mercy to her. He introduces her to the Fountain of Living Water as she drops her water pot to become one! May the Lord open our eyes to see the **Well** of the Living One who sees us!

The last two verses tell of Abram naming his son. Finally, at 86, Abram has a son, Ishmael. Perhaps Hagar never told Abram the name God had given her in the wilderness. What a shock this would have been to her when Abram chooses the name Ishmael ('God hears'). Abram may have assumed that God had heard his cry for a son and honored the work of the flesh to give birth to the child of promise. If so, Abram was mistaken. Abram and Sarai had further yet to go in their faith. Sarai is still barren, and the son of promise has not yet arrived....

"No longer will you be called Abram; your name will be Abraham, or I have made you a father of many nations."
Genesis 17:5

Chapter Five

THE ALL-SUFFICIENT GOD!
"I AM GOD ALMIGHTY;
WALK BEFORE ME AND BE BLAMELESS."

Before grace steps in, Abram must come to the end of himself. He was 75 when he left Haran. Ishmael was born when he was 86. Thirteen years later God appears again to his broken servant to reaffirm His oath that the son of promise will be born. Thirteen is the number in Scripture that represents unbelief, apostasy, and rebellion. For 13 years God did not appear to Abraham.

Why must God's people wait so long for the promise of God to be fulfilled? Why must so many years drag their weary course before God 'came through' for Abraham? Before 'God the Sufficient-One' displays His power we must see how insufficient we are in ourselves. Not until Abraham's body was as good as *"dead"* (Rom. 4:19) did God fulfill His Word and give him a son. God's sense of timing is related to our character formation. Every delay has a purpose to it. When we give up, God is ready to act. (Psalm 107)!

41

God revealed Himself to Abram as **"God Almighty"** or El Shaddai, 'the All Sufficient God.' The literal Hebrew is, 'the God of the breast, the Nourisher, the Sustainer.' The name El Shaddai is the most frequently used name of God before the giving of the Law by Moses. It reveals God as the Strengthener and Sustainer of His people. God All-Sufficient would be perhaps the best way to convey the meaning of the Hebrew. He not only enriches and protects, but He makes fruitful. To a man 99 years of age, *God All-Sufficient* promises to give Him a son and keep all His promises.

A fresh revelation of God is before Abram — **"I Am God Almighty! Walk before Me and be blameless!"** This was a new challenge to Abram. How would you like to receive a prophetic word that you were to walk before God blameless? How about if it was God Himself who appeared to you with this word? Would it shake you? Would it challenge you? Does it seem impossible?

This is the heart standard we must all go for. This is the mark of the high calling of God in Christ (Phil. 3:12–14). Remember, it is El Shaddai, the Almighty God who speaks this word. *His Name is our power.* Because He is Almighty, we can walk blamelessly. Only as we rest in the All-Sufficient God are we strengthened to purity.

It takes **Omnipotence** to change the heart of man. Only God is **All** Sufficient to lead us into voluntary surrender. Unbelief will rise and whisper of our weakness. Doubts will declare our history of failures. Self will speak up and remind us of our short-lived resolutions and broken vows. It is You alone, God Almighty, who can break my heart and turn me from sin!

"Walk before Me" — this is true freedom; to be free from the false self that walks before others. This means to have nothing before our hearts but God Himself. If I have my expectations upon others ... I am not walking before God. If I have my expectations in things

... I am not walking before God. If I expect good things from me...
I am not walking before God. **Who** or **What** do you have before
you as the object of your heart? Does God entirely fill your future?
Your present? Faith fills the heart with God, leaving no room for the
world. *"He alone is my Rock and my Salvation"* (Ps. 62:5–6).

God's leaders must be those who have the grace for a blameless
walk (I Tim. 3:2). A blameless walk is not the same as perfection,
for only God is holy. A blameless heart carries failure to the cross.
To be blameless means we have seen our need but see grace as
greater than our fall. We carry no sin, for Jesus carried it on our
behalf. Blameless means free from the burden of sin. There is no
accusation that abides when we walk blameless before Him.

Abram fell on his face and God talked with him! It is when
man is in the dust that God can speak in grace. Abram's posture is
a picture of his heart being broken before this revelation of God.
Abram becomes a worshipper, bowing low before the presence of
God. He is given the name **Abraham, "father of many** (nations)."
A change of name in Scripture is equivalent to a change of heart.
It takes a revelation of God All-Sufficient to truly change the
heart of a man. His power effects lasting transformation in our
character. From this day forward **Abraham** would be his name.
He would see himself in the light of God. The work of God has
brought it pass.

He will now be a world-changer, a father of many! Abram
means 'exalted father' and Abraham means 'father of a multitude.'
If you had a choice of being exalted or being multiplied, which
would you choose? Instead of being highly exalted to the highest
place, would you choose to be flattened, broken, and multiplied?
To be multiplied is to have more children — more troubles.
Everyone likes being exalted, but God's plan is to multiply us. This
change of name signals a change of heart for Abraham. God wants
to be expressed through Abraham's multiplication, not through

Abraham's exaltation. The church today does not need exalted fathers — we need fathers who will multiply themselves in their sons. A generational transfer is in the heart of God and revealed to Abraham.

➢ I Will make you very fruitful.

➢ I Will make nations of you, kings will come from you.

➢ I Will establish my covenant — an everlasting covenant.

➢ I Will give you the whole land of Canaan.

➢ I Will be their God.

➢ I Will establish my covenant with Isaac.

➢ I Will give you a son, Isaac by this time next year

CIRCUMCISION, ISAAC, & ISHMAEL (17:9–27)

There must be no exception — every member of the household of faith must bear the seal of that covenant. This speaks of **Cutting Away Of The Flesh** to walk in new creation life.[11] Circumcision was the sign or the seal of the Abrahamic Covenant (Rom. 4). Those who were circumcised would now be identified with Abraham's Covenant. In Exodus we learn how much this sign meant to God (Ex. 4:24–26). Moses was going to be killed if he did not circumcise his son! The outward sign of circumcision was the only thing God required from Abraham and his descendants. The spiritual counterpart is the cutting away of the flesh from the heart of man (Rom.2:28–29, Col.3:11). God's people were to be set apart for Him alone (Deut.30:6). Our flesh is laid aside to pursue the heavenly ways of God Most High.

Circumcision relates to the secret part of the body — for true circumcision is of the heart. God sought to carve into the body the truth that man must not live for self but for God. The very flesh that produced Ishmael must be cut away. The Creator wanted a new 'heart relationship' with man (Gal. 6:15). God wants to do more than change your goals.... He wants to end your life!

Sarai now has her name changed to Sarah — **'Princess.'** She will become a mother of many nations, a mother of kings, a 'Princess' with God. Abraham falls before God and laughs over the impossibility of Sarah bearing a child. This had never happened before. Sarah was well past childbearing age — she was 90. How could a 90-year-old woman and a 100-year-old man have a child? Parents and child would both be using walkers! It is humorous indeed. Not only would she have a son, nations and kings would come from her.

Abraham said, **"If only Ishmael might live under your blessing."** It seems that he was asking God if there was some way all of this could just come to Ishmael. Would not it be easier just to use Ishmael; he is already here. Abraham was asking God to take a shortcut. The fallen heart of man does not want to be broken. We would rather God just change us a little and use our flesh (our Ishmael) instead of falling on the rock and being broken. We become defensive when God uses others to reveal our flesh for what it is. Ishmael's nature was a wild donkey — he could not be the "seed" promised to Abraham. There must be a new source of life ... **Isaac** must be the heir.

God gives Abraham the name of his son, **Isaac**, which means, 'he laughs.' The naming of the child Isaac was to be a reminder of Abraham's laughter — the joining of faith and doubt seen in his laugh. As for Ishmael, God also promises a blessing to come upon him. Ishmael would likewise become a great nation. This demonstrates that God's blessings from the beginning are not only to Israel, but also for **All** the nations of the earth.

MESSENGERS FROM HEAVEN (18:1–15)

The Lord again **"appears"** to Abraham, His friend. How kind was the Lord to come to this man over and over again. At first, God appeared to Abraham as the God of Glory. Then He showed up as the Most High God — Possessor of Heaven and Earth. Later He came as El Shaddai ... and now He comes as a mortal man ... As a Friend.

If the Lord were to come to you, which way would you prefer? Should He come as the God of Glory and terrify you? Or, as The Most High God ... leaving you uneasy and uncomfortable? What if He were to come to you as a Friend and let you wash his feet? Which would be more pleasant ... for Him to sit on His throne and demand you bow the knee to Him in worship? Or for God to sit as your Friend under a shade tree with you as you refresh His heart?

Long before Mary of Bethany washed Jesus' feet with her tears, Abraham washed His feet in front of his tent door.... What sweet intimacy we see in this chapter! Three times in Scripture we are told that God made Abraham His friend. In II Chron. 20:7, God is the one who gave the land to Abraham, His friend. In Isa. 41:8, God calls Abraham His friend and chosen one. And in James 2:23, because Abraham believed, he was called God's friend.

You too have been given an inheritance, since you believed. You are now His chosen friend. Friendship with God is the greatest treasure you have. Cultivate that friendship with extravagant worship and voluntary obedience. The Lord comes to His Covenant Friends and shares His heart with them. He comes not in majestic splendor, but in the familiarity and freedom of a Friend.

This gives us a beautiful example of Revelation 3:20, *"Behold, I stand at the door and knock: if any man hear my voice, and open the door, I will come in to him, and dine with him...."* The Lord comes to dine with His friend. An obedient heart enjoys a communion that others know nothing of ... O, the joys of every intimate friend of God:

➤ Abraham provided refreshment *For* the Lord.

➤ Abraham enjoyed full communion *With* the Lord.

➢ Abraham interceded for others **Before** the Lord.

"**The Lord appeared to Abraham near the great trees of Mamre while he was sitting at the entrance to his tent in the heat of the day.**" Abraham was looking for his day of visitation in the place of fellowship (Hebron) under the anointing (Mamre = fatness). He sat at the entrance of his tent, gazing, looking, and longing. When he saw the three men coming, he ran to them. He was ready, anticipating, expecting. This friend of God wanted a visitation. One of these men was none other than the Lord Jesus in human form.

"**Abraham looked up and saw three men standing nearby. When he saw them, he hurried from the entrance of his tent to meet them and bowed low to the ground.**" Two different words are used here for "looked" and "saw." Abraham "saw" with spiritual vision three men coming to him. In verse 2, it says that he "looked," which means visual sight, and he "saw" them with spiritual sight. It means that he discerned there was something different about these three people[12] and ran to bow down before them. Abraham knew it was his day of visitation, bowing low in worship before this **Man**.

The word for bow is also translated in the Old Testament as 'worship.' This is the first time it appears in the Bible. Isn't it unusual that in its first appearance it refers to one bowing down and worshiping God in human form?

Abraham was a hospitable man. The sheiks and Bedouins of that time were known for hospitality. Historians say that many of the Bedouins and sheiks prepare their meals and eat in their tent flaps so if someone happens to come by they can invite him to come over and eat with them. After all his unusual experiences, Abraham knows by now that anything can happen. Knowing that this might be something new about to happen, he does not take any chances but invites them in. He is ready for anything.

He begged the Lord saying, "**Do not pass your servant by.**" He wanted the Divine Guest to remain and abide with him. He offers to wash their feet and to refresh them with food. Abraham was not about to miss this one — he wanted the Lord to stay with him. After the Lord said 'Yes', Abraham ran back to the tent to tell Sarah to fix a meal. Bread was baked and a tender calf was prepared with curds and milk. This would have taken some time and great deal of work, but in a Day of Visitation, there is no price too great to be with Him!

Abram served them a rich meal of three cakes of fine wheat flour baked over embers, a tender calf,[13] with butter and milk. In both Genesis 18 and Matthew 13:33, three measures ('seahs') of fine flour signify the resurrected humanity of Christ — His life in the believer. Your Lord Jesus is like the finest of flour baked into cakes and served as food both to God and man.

God came to have lunch with Abraham. **He** ate Sarah's cooking. God and the angels also ate butter and milk. God was the first to drink the milk of the Promised Land, long before the children of Israel did! The cakes of bread, the tender calf, the butter, the milk — it all speaks of the riches of the wonderful Son of God, the Christ who satisfies both God and man! In principle, Abram offers all of this as a sacrifice to God![14]

Whenever we are in fellowship with God, communing with Him as our Friend we are offering back to Him the riches of **His Life** and sacrifice for us. We never really offer sacrifice, we only offer back to God the sacrifice of His Son. We offer Him back to God for His enjoyment. God ate the sacrifice Abram offered to Him!

Abraham served his guests himself, standing near them under the tree. Waiting and ready, this giant of the faith becomes a servant and washes the feet of these Guests. What a picture this was. God had come down as a Man to spend time with His Friend. Jesus dined with His friend in a Covenant Meal (Rev. 3:20).

The Lord Jesus loves to come incognito into the homes of those He cherishes. If Jesus would come to us in His Manifest Presence with Glory and Splendor we would all recognize Him. Often He will visit us as a homeless stranger, a wayfaring man hungry and thirsty.... One who seeks refreshment from us. We may pass right by Him not knowing Him as the sick one, or the prisoner, or the foreigner. In whatever disguise He comes to us we must be ready, treating every human being with respect and compassion (Matt. 25:45).

After the meal, the conversation began. They first ask, **"Where is your wife, Sarah?"** That question tells us that these are heavenly visitors. Otherwise, how would they have known Abraham was married? How did they know his wife's name was *Sarah*? Her name had always been Sarai. Had they not been heavenly visitors, they would not have known of the name change, which had taken place immediately preceding this event.

What a confirmation to Abraham's heart! The Lord Himself comes down and tells him, **"Sarah shall have a son!"** It is though God wanted to 'hand deliver' the birth announcement! Sarah overheard this and laughed to herself just like Abraham did. Yet she denied it out of fear. Fear makes cowards out of us all. It is faith that makes us truthful and confident. Sarah's faith was born at that moment. When she knew her laughter had been discovered she was suddenly filled with godly fear. Sarah was laughing at God. For the first time she realized that God was at work behind the scenes. She was not laughing now; she believed!

It is important to note that Sarah's folly (Ishmael) did not remove her from God's purpose for her life. God does not give up on us when we fail. He took it all into consideration when He chose us. Even her laughing at God would not change His mind! He was determined to finish what He began in her heart until she saw His glory. We are all like Sarah. We manipulate prophecy and judge His promises to be impossible. We laugh inwardly even thinking about our inability to change. However, God is as kind to us as He was with Sarah. He still includes us in His Divine Purpose.

One year from now we may look back and see impossibility turn into destiny!

The Lord makes a statement that should sink deep into every faithful heart — **"Is anything too hard for the Lord?"** There is nothing you are facing right now that the Lord is not sufficient for. The Hebrew is literally — 'Is anything too **Marvelous** for the Lord?' This same Hebrew word is used as a title of the Lord Jesus in Isaiah 9:6 (*"Wonderful"*). Nothing is too extraordinary for God! He is Wonderful! This question remained unanswered for 3,000 years until Jeremiah the prophet responds; "There is nothing too hard for You! (Jer. 32:17)! He delights in doing what is impossible to man. This child would be known as the Lord's provision.

"By faith Abraham, even though he was past age — and Sarah herself was barren — was enabled to become a father because he considered him faithful who had made the promise." Heb.11:11

How big is God? How hard is it for Him to answer your prayer and deliver you from trouble? Nothing can be compared to God's marvelous power. He has all that is needed to make the prophetic word happen. There is no match for Him! Num.11:23, Matt.19:16, Mk 10:27.

"Then the Lord said, "The outcry against Sodom and Gomorrah is so great and their sin so grievous that I will go down and see if what they have done is as bad as the outcry that has reached me...." Genesis 18:20–21

---

[11] Eight is the number of new beginnings.

[12] Perhaps the other two visitors were angels. Those who are careful to entertain strangers may be welcoming angels unawares (Heb.13:2).

[13] Abram also prepared the fatted calf, which is what the father in Luke 15 gave to his "prodigal" son when he returned in repentance.

[14] See Leviticus 1 & 2 where the prescribed offerings are the very things Abraham and Sarah serve their guests. These sacrifices in Leviticus were ordered 560 years after the time of Abraham. God had come to dine with his friend....

Chapter Six

ABRAHAM THE INTERCESSOR
"THEN THE LORD SAID, "SHALL I HIDE FROM ABRAHAM WHAT I AM ABOUT TO DO?"

hat was the message God came to deliver to Abram? The birth of Isaac and the destruction of Sodom. Isaac must come and Sodom must go. Every time Christ comes in, sin must go out. He did not just come to speak judgment over Sodom — He came to reaffirm the promise of a son. It is always the manifestation of Christ (Isaac the son) that will destroy the works of Sodom (I John 3:8). He intends to produce the Christ in us and destroy the 'Sodom' in our soul.

As the three men begin to walk off toward Sodom, Abraham ventures along with them. How we want to linger with the Lord when His presence is near. The more closely we walk with Jesus, the more of His heart He will share with us. Walking along with His friend Abraham, the Lord begins to share His secrets about what He is about to do (Ps. 25:14, John 15:15). This is the key to prophetic revelation; walking close to Jesus, pursuing Him while He is near. As you cultivate friendship with Jesus, he will not hold back from you.

"Shall I hide from Abraham what I am about to do?" The Lord describes Abraham as a man who will direct his children after him, instructing them to keep the way of the Lord. He would be a good father, a good example. The Father saw in Abraham a father's heart, willing to make a generational transfer to his sons.[15] For this reason, God was moved as a Father, to share His secrets with the patriarch.

The Lord wants the righteous (and our children) to understand His just decisions. If we are to teach others the ways of God — we must be acquainted with them firsthand. He informs Abraham that He is on a mission to see how evil and grievous the sin of Sodom is. The other two men (angels) go off to Sodom as Abraham and the Lord stand face to face....

"Abraham remained standing before the Lord." Here was the Friend of God waiting to fellowship with the Lord. And what did Abraham do with these Divine secrets? Did he tell the Lord how right He was to judge Sodom because of what his lousy nephew did? He took this information to the Lord in intercession. Abraham became an intercessor — pleading for the city of Sodom.

Abraham approached God! He drew near to his Divine Visitor. He came up close *"like a prince"* (Job 31:37) to look face-to-face before this Man from Heaven. Abraham devoted himself to be close to God (Jer. 30:21). Why did he draw near? To stand in the gap for others! Hearts enlarged by personal communion with God will take in more of His grace for others.

The sinfulness of man challenging the holiness of God was the **"outcry"** for judgment. Something must be done with this wicked city. Yet, even sharing this with Abraham was an indirect invitation for him to intercede. Abraham's mind was filled with a tumult of emotion. Abraham's heart was broken for his brother's son — and a wayward city. He had rescued them himself once, now he begins to plead with the Lord to spare them. Abraham **Knew** they deserved judgment — but he could not understand how God would destroy the righteous and the wicked together. Moving in faith, Abraham boldly spoke to God for those facing judgment. This is true intercession.

His lonely prayer for the lost moved God's heart. As they stood together overlooking the city, just the two of them, Abraham humbly reasoned with the Lord. Realizing he was only **"dust and ashes"** standing before Omnipotence — he pleaded, **"Will not the Judge of all the earth do right?"** God was not angry with this. He wanted this plea to come before Him. Abraham prayed not to move God's heart but to express His heart!

What if there are **50** righteous? **45? 40? 30? 20? 10?** Six times[16] Abraham asked the Lord for mercy. Each time **God** was drawing him out. What if Abraham dared asked for only **One** righteous; would God still destroy the city? What a pity he stopped at 10!

Although judgment fell from heaven — the **Mercy** of God is **Above** the heavens. God stopped when man stopped. God waited for an intercessor and limited Himself to the requests of the intercessor (Isa. 59:16, Ezek. 23:30–31). When we think we have asked our limit, there are more resources of mercy that God would release for us!

God will deliver a city for the sake of one, yes, even one: *"Go up and down the streets of Jerusalem, look around and consider, search through her squares. If you can find but one person who deals honestly and seeks the truth, I will forgive this city."* Jer. 5:1

Man always thinks he has exhausted the mercy of God. We are afraid we have overstepped our bounds. Yet His piercing mercy is boundless, higher than the heaven. We can never expect too much from God. This interchange warmed the heart of God as He heard Abraham crying out for mercy....

This passage is one of the highlights of the Old Testament as an example of intercessory prayer. In Genesis 15:2, Abram said, "O *Lord God, what will thou give me since I am childless?"* Verse 8: "O *Lord God, how may I know that I shall possess it?"* In 17:18: *"O that Ishmael might live before thee."* In Genesis 18 he begins to pray, not for those things that are self-centered; he reaches out and prays for Lot and for the other righteous that he thought would be in the city. He also prays for the cities themselves. He prays for relatives, for other righteous people not relatives whom Lot should have won to the Lord, and then for the cities themselves....

In terms of intercessory prayer, this incident is still phase one in Abraham's life. Later, in chapter 20, he is instructed to pray for the unrighteous. We see a growing development in his life: first praying for himself, then interceding for other righteous people, then going a step further, being instructed to pray for someone who is an unbeliever. An entire city would have been spared if there are 10 righteous in it. **Intercessors** — this is a principle of Divine government that **You** can implement in your intercession for the cities of the earth. We can do more than watch the slide of the world into darkness; we can avert judgment by our prayers.

Here's the formula: We know that if there are only **Ten Righteous** in a city that God will deliver that city *if* there is intercession coming before Him! Even though the cry of wickedness is great in our cities today, the Lord is willing to spare them for the sake of the righteous.

Abraham did not change the mind of God; he demonstrated it ... Abraham knew God so well that he knew there was a mercy string to pluck in the heart of Father-God. Like Abraham, let us linger with our Lord long enough to plead for mercy.

FIRE & BRIMSTONE (GENESIS 19)

The chapter opens with Lot sitting at the gate of Sodom, the seat of authority, and ends with him in a cave. From councilman to caveman ... what a difference a day makes! Apparently, Lot had risen to prominence in this wicked place. How vain to achieve success in a world system that will someday be destroyed (I John 2:17). The world was his snare for twenty years as he dwelt in Sodom. He chose the city of Sodom over the tents of pilgrimage....

Abraham entertained heavenly visitors in chapter 18, and now Lot entertains them in chapter 19. Abraham was waiting for his visitation by the trees of Mamre (under the anointing) but Lot was sitting at the gate of Sodom. Lot walked in the counsel of the ungodly; Abraham walked with God. Lot stood in the path of sinners; Abraham stood in the path of God. Lot is seated in the seat of the scornful; Abraham sits and communes with God.[17] Has Lot lost his reason or his logic? He was rescued one time by Abraham's intervention, and now he is back there again.

The words of the angels to Lot were a condemnation of his lifestyle. They would rather dwell in the streets of Sodom than enter the house of a 'backslider' from God. Lot's insistence however, won them over. Soon the people of Sodom surrounded Lot's house, threatening to break in and rape the men. How low can man sink into sin! Lot offered his virgin daughters to the lusting mob. (The sin of homosexuality was so prevalent in Sodom that his married daughters were still virgins!) As the argument heated, the angels pulled Lot inside and struck the mob with blindness.

As Lot discovered who these men were and why they were sent, he hurriedly tried to convince his son-in-laws to flee out of the city. Unlike Noah, Lot was unable to convince his whole family that the warning was serious. How bound they were in wickedness! Refusing to leave they were destroyed with the wicked. Even intercession cannot save those who are determined to perish.

The angels had to literally drag Lot, his wife, and daughters out of Sodom. As they fled, Lot begged to stop at Zoar[18], a small city nearby. Not wanting to be too far from the city of doom, Lot was showing his true colors. He is telling God what he wants to do. It was foolish for Lot to pick his resting place when God wanted to take him to the mountaintop. Interestingly, the angels hurried Lot, for they could not destroy the city until the righteous had escaped. Even Zoar was spared as a city of refuge for Lot. How merciful is our God to spare the righteous, still bound by sin. The presence of the righteous will fend off the judgments of God (Rev. 7:3, Ezek. 9:4).

The sun rose that day just like any other. But the storm cloud of judgment had already formed. The Lord rained down burning sulfur upon the cities of Sodom and Gomorrah. The Life-Giver had become the Destroyer. Judgment was falling from the skies — smoke, fire, burning sulfur. The day of wrath had come for those who rejected Holiness. *"On the wicked He will rain fiery coals and burning sulfur; a scorching wind will be their lot (Ps. 11:6)."* Never had there been a day like this. Hell rained down from heaven. This judgment is a standing revelation of the wrath of God. On one day, 400 years after the flood, fire fell from heaven. The *vengeance* of eternal fire will come to all that live ungodly.

The entire human race is under the wrath of God. It is His righteous judgment against unrepentant sin. One day, the place of the damned will be an eternal lake of fire as Divine Justice glorifies itself. Let us learn from this ... behold the terror of the Lord (II Cor. 5:11)!

Lot's wife looked back at the judgment of the Lord and was turned into a pillar of salt, entombed where she stood. The sense of the Hebrew text is that she lingered behind the others, casting fond glances on what she was leaving. In so doing she was caught in the eruption. Even our Lord Jesus referred to this (Luke 12:32). Just as the destruction of Sodom and Gomorrah serve as an example of what happens to the wicked, so by the example of Lot's wife we see what happens to the righteous if they turn back from their righteousness. She disobeyed and was judged.

Her backward gaze showed that she wanted what she left; her heart longed to go back. Let us not be those who draw back unto judgment (Heb. 4:1). Lot's wife did not fall over dead; she froze into a pillar — a **Monument!** This pillar of salt should season us. Let us **Always** press forward to the prize of the high calling of God (Phil. 3:13–14).

Jesus made it clear that if the miracles He did in Israel had been seen in Sodom, they would have repented. Because of this, it will be more tolerable for them in the Day of Judgment than for the cities of Galilee (Matt.11:20–24). It is clear how we should then live; knowing how God will soon judge the corrupt world around us (II Pet. 3:11–15).

Early that morning, the intercessor, Abraham, got up and returned to his *"watchtower"* (Hab. 2:1) to see what would happen to Sodom. From this elevated place he saw the smoke of judgment rising in the sky like a belching furnace. It was for the sake of Abraham that God delivered Lot from the catastrophe that destroyed the cities of the plain. A similar scene will take place as the smoke of Babylon's torment rises up forever and ever (Rev. 19:3).

Lot finally left Zoar and went up into the mountains in a cave. The safest place for Lot would be to return in repentance to Abraham, dwelling under his anointing. Lot was not wise enough to know what was best. While dwelling in the cave with his two daughters, a scheme was hatched. The daughters contrived to sleep with their father, to propagate the family name. Lot had no sons, the daughters had no husbands. Making him drunk with wine, they slept with him, the oldest one night, and the youngest the next. Whatever their pretense, their plan was vile. Having witnessed the judgment of God upon the wicked, they just didn't seem to get it.

How could the fires of lust burn in them when they had witnessed Sodom's flames?

Two sons (or grandsons) came from these incestuous conceptions, Moab ('son of the father'), and Ammon ('son of the nearest kinsman'). They became the fathers of two nations that became determined enemies of God's people. Molech was an Ammonite deity. Grace however, included Ruth, a Moabitess (Ruth 1:4), a descendant of Lot through his daughter, in the family line of Jesus Christ (Matt.1:3–5). Is this not the far-reaching mercy of God?

"But God came to Abimelech in a dream one night and said to him, "You are as good as dead because of the woman (Sarah) you have taken; she is a married woman." Genesis 20:3

---

[15] To receive a covenant is not only receiving a new responsibility, but an obligation to release its power to multiple generations to come.

[16] Six is the number of man ... what would have happened if Abraham had asked the seventh time? But Abraham stopped at six times and ten people.

[17] See Psalm 1.

[18] Zoar means 'small.' An escape mentality will make us run from the mess, but will take us to a small box where our dreams die and we protect our turf. The path of escapism is a path to 'Smallville' — the place of self-preservation!

A DETOUR, A DREAM, A BABY

"ABIMELECH ASKED, 'WHAT WAS YOUR REASON FOR DOING THIS?'"

Ancient Jewish historians tell us that Abraham left Mamre (the place of 'fatness') to go into the country of the Philistines because of the mocking of his neighbors. Again Abraham moves his tents and journeys to Gerar. The king of Gerar, Abimelech, seeing Sarah, took her into his household. Abraham lies by telling the king she was his sister. Nevertheless, the Lord would not forsake him.

God came to Abimelech one night in a dream and warned him of the consequences for taking another man's wife. How many times has God done this to the wayward ones — warned them of adultery? This pagan king heeded the warning. Why don't we (Job 33:14–18)?

We see from this that God does not only speak in dreams to the righteous, He will also come to the lost and share His heart with them (Prov.21:1). Dreams are powerful avenues into the spirit of man. God will speak to you in dreams, if you will listen.

Abimelech pleads his innocence to God in the dream, for Sarah and Abraham had assured him that she was his sister. Because of his ignorance, God preserves Abimelech from committing adultery with Sarah. God's restraining hand kept this from happening. It is a great mercy to be hindered by God from sinning (I Sam. 25:32–33). God commands Abimelech to restore Sarah to her husband and ask Abraham to pray for him.

God calls Abraham a prophet who will pray for healing and restoration. This is the true definition of a prophet. Not only one who speaks for God — but one who will intercede and pray for man to be restored to God. There is great power in the prayer of a prophetic intercessor. You are wise to have a prophet pray for you.

God does not need our lies to protect us. Abraham tried to clear himself by telling Abimelech that Sarah was his half-sister. Regardless, Abraham lied because he feared man. Twenty-five years earlier Abraham had fallen in the same sin. God will bring out the evil in our hearts so we can see ourselves for what we are. Peter could not have believed that he would deny the Lord until circumstances brought out the evil that was there. God arranges stress points to come, to reveal our weaknesses. His strategy is humble us; bringing us to Him.

God closed the womb of every woman in Abimelech's household, including his servants. By Abraham's intercession, they were healed. This is amazing considering that Abraham's wife had never given him a child! The very first healing in the Bible was through the prayer of a childless man, Abraham. He had no confidence in himself as he prayed this prayer of faith. He could pray in total confidence that it **Had** to be God doing the miracle. Abraham paid a price for the women of Abimelech. He prayed for the thing he had not received.

Praying for someone else when you are sick is sowing a seed for your own healing! When God healed Abimelech's household it was a catalyst for faith for Abraham's household. When the last two verses of Genesis 20 are read with the first two verses of Genesis 21, we see that Isaac's conception occurred as a result of Abraham's prayer for another person with an identical need. Perhaps this is what James meant when he tells us to *"pray for each other so that you* [all] *may be healed."* James 5:16

Again, we see Abraham blessed materially, even in the place of compromise. Abimelech gave him royal gifts of sheep, cattle, servants, and one thousand shekels of silver (25 pounds!) to cover his offense against them. They left richer than what they came! In the restoration of Sarah, we see a picture of the restoration of the church. Sarah was rejuvenated between chapters 18 and 20. She was past the age of childbirth in 18, but in 19 she is so beautiful that a king desires her! Either the king was blind or a miracle happened! This transformation came in one year because she believed the word of the Lord (Heb. 11:11). Truth in her inward parts now brought healing — revitalization! Fragments from the Dead Sea scrolls describe Sarah as the most attractive of women — at 90 years old!

THE MIRACLE BABY! (GEN. 21:1–8)

The appointed time had arrived. God had kept His Word. He was gracious to Sarah. No Word of God will fall to the ground unfulfilled. He is faithful even when we doubt. Nothing can hinder God when it is time for a miracle — is anything too hard for the Lord? So often our wise Father waits until boasting turns to prayer. It is when we are without strength that God moves on our behalf (Rom. 5:6). He will wait until we are powerless. The miracle must be God, for our strength has failed. The Lord delights to do this. We must always remember, God is **Never** in a hurry. It is His Divine sense of humor to wait until 11:59!

Isaac was his name — 'laughter.' Every time they called their son, they were reminded of how God pulled it off! Laughter filled their home as they recounted the miracle birth of their son. He would be the joy of all nations — blessed through him. When Isaac was eight days old he was circumcised, establishing God's covenant with Abraham and his seed. Abraham was 100 years old before he had a son with Sarah — what a wait! It makes our impatience seem petty. Wait, servant of the Lord. His Word will come to pass! Happy you will be when God makes you laugh!

Sarah rejoiced over this son of promise. She prophesied that others would laugh with her when they hear the news. Sarah, a 90 year old woman nursing a child! Funny, isn't it! In time, Isaac was weaned and his father threw a great feast to celebrate the occasion. The milk gives way to meat (Heb. 5:11–14). Isaac is a type of Christ who was also born in due time (Gal. 4:4). Notice the details of Isaac's birth and how they foreshadow the birth of our Lord Jesus:

1. Both were the promised seed. Gen.17:6, Isa.7:14
2. Both were long awaited. Gen.12:7, 21:1–3, Gal.4:4
3. Both had mothers who asked questions. Gen.28:13–14, Lk.1:34–37
4. Both had names signified before birth. Gen.17:9, Matt.1:21
5. Both births were miraculous. Gen.21:2, Matt.1:18
6. Both were a delight to their father. Gen.21:3, Matt.3:17

HAGAR AND ISHMAEL SENT AWAY (21:9–21)

Jealousy was a continual battle in the house of Abraham. As Sarah observed Hagar and Ishmael mocking her son, she could stand their ridicule no longer. Paul used the word *"persecute"* to describe what took place (Gal. 4:29). The counterfeit will always persecute the ordained. Sarah insisted that Abraham expel their servant and her son. Abraham was grieved over this matter, but God approved of Sarah's plan. Isaac was confirmed by God to be the true *"heir."*

As soon as Isaac comes, Ishmael must go. It is time to cast out the bondwoman and her son. The casting out of Ishmael is a picture of the believer 'casting off' the works of the flesh, our Ishmael. As Isaac grew (Christ must increase) Ishmael must leave (I/flesh must decrease). As Hagar and Ishmael fled, they wandered into a desert area where there was no apparent water supply. Mocking the purpose of God will take you to a wilderness.

God heard the cry of Ishmael and directed them to a source of water, a well. God is the God of the outcast. He is the God of the rejected, the abused, and the forgotten. Here was an unfortunate woman caught in the web of Abraham and Sarah's efforts to achieve their destiny. Hagar was suddenly very much in the way. But God would not let them die in the wilderness; he rescued them and gave them a new life. God heard the intercession for Hagar's son.

This narrative is interpreted by Paul in Galatians 3–5 as the struggle with flesh and the Spirit. The flesh will always trust in works (the Law) and the Spirit is always released by faith. Hagar represents the bondage of Sinai, Sarah the freedom of the promise. Once the promise if fulfilled, the old order must be done away with (driving out Hagar and Ishmael). Ishmael cannot become the heir.

THE COVENANT AT BEERSHEBA (21:22–34)

The root of failure was now removed. God would fully manifest His work through Isaac. Even Abimelech saw that God was with Abraham, fulfilling His purpose in his life. A covenant is made with Abraham and Abimelech, allowing Abraham to settle in the land in peace. The Philistines knew that God was with Abraham and that he had authority to bless. In Abraham, God blesses the nations.

Abraham took this opportunity to bring up an issue that was dear to him — the well! Everywhere that Abraham went, he dug a well and built an altar. Fellowship with God at the well — no one was to interfere with this. He pressed his case with Abimelech and they confirmed their treaty with an oath. Abimelech returned the well to the one who dug it and Abraham gave him seven ewe lambs. The place was called Beersheba ('the place of seven wells' or 'the well of the oath').

Seven lambs would mean a well for each lamb. The well for Isaac, dug by Abraham, had been taken by force by Abimelech's servants. Now it was a redeemed well. At the cost of seven ewe lambs Abraham redeemed this well for Isaac. These seven lambs signify the full, complete, and perfect redemption of Jesus Christ that has released **Living Water** to His redeemed ones. In the midst of a world that lives without a source of living water, we are living by a redeemed source. The water we drink as believers is not natural but supernatural; purchased by the blood of the **Lamb**. We drink His water of life and enter into **Covenant** with Him forever! With a redeemed well Abraham enters a period of rest as he dwells in the land of the Philistines in peace. This is where Isaac was raised.

Abraham planted a tamarisk tree, a type of willow that often grows near water. In Genesis 2 there was a Tree of Life in the Garden of Eden. In this garden of Beersheba, Abraham planted a tamarisk tree that spoke of eternal life. The tamarisk tree was not for landscaping; it was a statement of faith. Planting the tree shows faith for endurance until the time of fruitfulness (Isa. 65:22). You and I are like that evergreen tree planted by a source of living water. His relationship with God deepens as has calls upon the Name of the Lord — The Eternal God.

Abraham receives a new revelation of God — He is the Ever Living One (evergreen), the Eternal God. The Hebrew word for this is 'El Olam.' Other translations render this, 'The Ageless One, the Hidden One, The Always God' (Ps. 90:2). This is much more than saying He is the Eternal God — it is a statement that He is God over Eternity, God over eternal things! Abraham experienced God as the Eternal One; the Mysterious One (Isa.40:28). Abraham's heart and focus is now turning to the God of Eternity. The things of the earth are growing meaningless to him. Abraham is being prepared to yield his greatest treasure, his son. Only one whose heart is fixed on eternity can ever make sacrifices pleasing to God. When we see the Eternal One, we are able to let go of temporary things. Abraham touched eternal life as he dwelt by the tamarisk tree and the well. This was the true preparation for giving up Isaac. May we speak and sing to our well (Num. 21:17)!

"Then God said, "Take your son, your only son, Isaac, whom you love, and go to the region of Moriah. Sacrifice him there as a burnt offering on one of the mountains I will tell you about."
Genesis 22:2

Chapter Eight

ABRAHAM'S GREATEST TEST
"NOW I KNOW THAT YOU FEAR GOD."

After years of communion with God … and years of tests and trials, Abraham now endures the test of a lifetime. Would he offer up his son of promise? He let go of his plan for Ishmael, now he must yield up his Isaac. God was testing his loyalty, proving his sincerity, and refining his faith. Doesn't this happen to you? Doesn't God test your faith and your loyalty to Him? Have you ever had to let go of something that was dear to you? Has God ever challenged you to let go of *your* 'Isaac'? We all want the faith of Abraham but will we pass the tests of Abraham?

Abraham and Isaac have enjoyed sweet years of fellowship with El Olam at the well of Beersheba. Life was good. He had his son, he lived by the well, he planted a tree, and he walked with God.… Now the Lord came with a new word.

"Take your son, your only son, Isaac, whom you love...."

God plunged the knife into Abraham's soul when he heard these words. The Lord has an absolute claim upon our lives. As our Maker and King He has the right to demand from us anything that He pleases. Everything we have comes from Him.... We only give back to Him what has come from His hand (I Chron. 29:16). There are times that our God will come and tell us it is time to give back to Him what He has loaned us for a season. If we have thanked Him for what He has given, we must thank Him when He comes to take it back.

No mortal man in the Bible was tested like Abraham. His most beloved son, *Isaac*, the one Abraham waited all his life to have ... the son in whom all his hopes and prophetic words found their fulfillment. Isaac must be given to God! Would Abraham love God more than his son? There is no greater test to a father than to offer his son as a sacrifice to God. Yet this is God's way of perfecting faith. He promises us a destiny ... we wait until it is fulfilled, then He visits us with this question, *'Would you let go of this for Me?'*

One of the ways to translate "test" could be 'lift up.' This test was an opportunity for Abraham to be lifted up higher in his devotion and love for God. How meaningful is our every test, if only we could see it as God's ladder, His escalator to take us higher in the fires of sacrificial love! We all want Abraham's faith, but do we want Abraham's trial to perfect our faith?

God is behind our proving. The heart becomes His threshing floor as He sifts wheat from chaff. He does so to prove our love and test our devotion — not to destroy but to refine. When God proves us in this manner it is a sign that He is dealing **Intimately** with us. He sees what others do not. He sees not only the negative things we are ashamed of; He sees the virtues that **He** is bringing to maturity. Trials are God's vote of confidence of our future. The budding qualities of Christ-likeness are brought forth in every test of our faith. Someday, you may call a 'blessing' what you once called a 'burden.'

Every word God spoke here is a sword to Abraham's bones. The heart must be probed to the very bottom. **"Take your son"**, not your lambs or doves, your son! Abraham would have given thousands of lambs to preserve his son. **"Your only son"**, or his only son by Sarah. Ishmael had been cast out, must Isaac be given too? **"Isaac"**, the son of promise, the son of laughter. **"Whom you love"**, the beloved son of his old age. The son of miracle power....

Can you see God's open heart of love for **His Son** in this account? Jesus is the **Only Beloved** of the Father's heart. He spared not His own Son (Rom. 8:32). Can you imagine the emotion of that moment? God's sword goes deep into Abraham's heart. And so will that sword someday visit us. The love of God is a jealous fire that can have no rivals. There is a place in God where all other loves are like hatred compared to the fire of passion for God burning in our hearts. Until it consumes us, the sword of testing comes to challenge our faith. May we be found faithful in the day of testing. May we see the hands of Wisdom and Love behind each trial of our faith. In that hour we must say, "Here I am."

"Sacrifice him there as a burnt offering"

Moriah. The Temple of Solomon was built upon Mt. Moriah (II Chron. 3:1). It was also the site where David **Paid** a **Price** for Ornan's threshing floor (II Sam. 24, I Chron. 21). These two events teach us a lesson about God's ways. The Temple of the Lord will always be built at the place of sacrifice. It was to **Moriah** that Abraham must go to become the Temple of the Lord and the father of all who believe.

The name Moriah means 'the vision of Jah,' that is, 'the vision of Jehovah.' Moriah is where you see the Lord and the Lord sees you. Today we have a vision of the Lord on Mt. Zion, which is the church. There is no cloud there, for we are not in darkness, we are in the vision. Jehovah is seen every time we lay down an Isaac before Him. This mountain is the place of vision, and the place of provision. It is a vision of Jehovah-Jireh....

"Early the next morning...."

Abraham had a heart of ready obedience. There is no mention of doubt, fear, or questions yet we presume there were many. What would Sarah say? What would Isaac say? This man of faith did not delay to obey the word of the Lord. As the sun began to rise, Abraham set out on the longest journey of his life.

True faith never stops to look at circumstances and take a poll to see if it is popular to obey God. Faith simply responds to the Words from His mouth. Faith acts on the Word and that word of grace enables us to do His will.

Abraham was to offer his son as a sacrifice. This is the first time in Scripture we see a shadow of God's request for a human sacrifice. God gave Abraham no reasons, only a command. Isaac is to be offered to God in place of a lamb. Isaac was the lamb of Abraham. Jesus is the Lamb of God.

"We will worship and then we will come back to you"

After a heart breaking three-day journey, Abraham sees Mt. Moriah in the distance ... Two young men, servants, had accompanied Abraham and Isaac to the foot of Mt. Moriah. These two were witnesses, seeing the son carrying the wood up the mountain. However, what happened on the mountaintop was to be seen only by the father and the son. There were two "thieves" crucified on Calvary next to Jesus. They saw Him carry His cross. But they were not permitted to see what transpired that day between the Father and His Son, the Christ of God.

Abraham carried the fire and the knife. Every one who follows in faith will carry the fire (passion) and the instrument of death to whatever stands in the way of absolute abandonment. Are you carrying the **Fire** and the **Knife?** It was God the Father who carried Divine Holiness and Divine Judgment against the sin of man. The Beloved Son was *"stricken by God, smitten by Him and afflicted (Isa. 53:4)."*

What took place on the mountain is described by Abraham as **"worship."** He did not say he and the lad were going to sacrifice, but to worship. Faith sees the greatest sacrifice as an act of worship. Sacrifice is what **We** do, but worship points us to God. Not what we give up, but what He receives — this is worship. Worship in spirit and in truth is giving to God the dearest treasure and calling it the delight of worship. Our eyes will not be on what we give up, but on Him.

Notice the words of this man of faith — *"We will come back to you."* Abraham told his servants that they would return together! But didn't Abraham know he was to give his son in sacrifice on the altar? Yes. However, he knew that God could raise him from the dead! This is the faith we see as they march up the mountain. Abraham is convinced God could raise back to life his son. Heb.11:17–19.

"God Himself will provide the lamb...."

These words have a double meaning. They tell us that God is the One who will provide the lamb, and they make known that the lamb was for "Himself." God alone could supply that which would satisfy Himself. Nothing of man could meet Divine requirements. If there is to be a sacrifice for sin, God must be the One to supply it. The Lamb would not just be provided by God, but also *for* God. God Himself would be the LAMB! This is God announcing the gospel to Abraham (Gal.3:8). There is only one scene in all of human history that surpasses this one....

Abraham binds the guiltless hands of his son to the altar. He sets the wood in order and prepares to offer Isaac as a burnt offering to Yahweh. His darling son, Sarah's laughter, the heir of promise, the church's hope.... With a fixed heart and eye toward heaven, Abraham tearfully lifts the knife over his son.... Here is an act of obedience so astonishing that it is a spectacle to men and angels. The voice of the angel of the Lord pierces the sanctity of that moment with a reprieve.... **"Do not lay a hand on the boy ... Now I know that you fear God, because you have not withheld from Me your son, your only son."**

Isaac is rescued. Now Abraham realizes it was only a test of his faith. Abraham proved that he loved God more than his prophetic destiny. It was proof positive that Abraham was a man of faith. What else could he do to show that God was first in his life? Grace triumphed over every passion of his heart. The supernatural bond of faith was greater than the natural bond of human affection. Another sacrifice is provided instead of Isaac ... But at another time on a hill like Moriah, God the Father did not spare His own Son, but freely sacrificed Him on Calvary's altar. This story opens our eyes to the heart of God. The eternal Father gave us His dearest treasure, His only Son, Jesus.

At just the right time, Abraham turned and saw a ram caught by its horns in a thicket nearby. Abraham's words to Isaac were prophetic; God provided Himself a sacrifice! A new name is given to this place, Jehovah-Jireh, *"The Lord Will Provide."* Let it be forever known that on the Mountain of the Lord it will be provided. The secret is to remain on the Mountain of the Lord! Remember ... this mountain is not a certain place but a certain confidence and place of total helplessness and dependence upon God.

Abraham's obedience led to a fresh revelation of God. How valuable is our testing if it brings us to know our Father. It is only when we are put to the test that we discover who God is. Without trials we are only walking in theories, after the trial we walk in personal communion with Him. As Abraham returned to Beersheba, he walked in the new understanding of God being enough. Do you realize that the "angel of the Lord" that spoke with Abraham was the One who someday would be caught in the 'thicket' of our sins and crucified for us? Jehovah truly provided for us so great a salvation!

Behind the testing of Abraham lies the wisdom of God. Notice these Divine principles:

1 *When God tests us, what He is requiring of us often makes no sense at the time.*

God's command to give up Isaac made no sense at all. This is why faith is needed. Wherever there is no understanding there must be faith. God will remove the props of human reasoning to test our heart to see if we will believe His Word alone. We must be those who thank Him at all times. Loving gratitude must loosen our hold on every cherished thing. You will never lose by giving up anything to God. Faith yields to God, even when it does not make sense.

2 *Faith is never brought to maturity without a measure of suffering attached.*

God will someday make you a person of extraordinary faith. Fear will not be a part of your life, for the tests of life will make you confident that God will provide everything. Even Jesus was made perfect through sufferings (Heb.2:10, 5:8, Acts 14:22). Faith will carry you through the most severe trial. Faith lives within the veil.

3 *We must obey the Holy Spirit even before we know all the details of what is involved.*

Abraham's failure in producing an 'Ishmael' was because he was not content to not know all the details of God's promise. God left Abraham hanging ... And He leaves you and I hanging too! We must not strike a bargain with God, 'Just tell me first where you are taking me, then I'll go.' We must be willing not to know where God is taking us. Obedience is always one moment at a time. Abraham could truly say, *"To obey is better than sacrifice."* See I Samuel 15:22

4   *Others may not be permitted to know what God is doing with us.*

Abraham left the two servants behind, he left Sarah behind, only he and God must see this test. Often God will bring you to the lonely place where others cannot intrude ... they wouldn't understand anyway!

5   *The worst suffering and most severe test may lie yet in the future.*

Abraham had been tested throughout his life. God sifted him and proved him. Yet it all was in preparation of this one final exam. One day you will be tested to the fullest ... let this confidence be yours just like it was Abraham's — "The **Lord** will provide!" God will make you into a "living sacrifice." Rom.12:1

6   *God will not allow us to go on with an unhealthy attachment to our family.*

This was an issue in Abraham's life from the beginning. He was reluctant to leave them all behind. His obedience on Moriah finally put this problem to rest. Many parents view their future wrapped up in their children instead of in the Lord alone. It is easy then, to manipulate their lives to fulfill our own dreams. We must constantly give our children to the Lord where they and we, will find the blessing of God.

"I Will Surely Bless You...."

The Lord gives another prophetic affirmation to this aged saint. The promise will never be taken from him, God is determined to bless Abraham, making his descendants as numerous as the stars in the sky (spiritual Israel) and as the sand on the seashore (natural Israel). Because Abraham was obedient to the point of giving his son, God would bless the world through him (James 2:21). The true descendants of Abraham are his "seed", his spiritual children. The "seed" has his life, *his life of faith.*

The Jews of Jesus' day couldn't understand that Abraham's "seed" was not guaranteed merely because they were born of Isaac (John 8:33). They must have the faith of Abraham if they are to be known as his "seed" (Rom. 9:6–8). The apostle Paul taught that a Jew was a *son of Ishmael* if they remained under the law and refuse to embrace God's promise of grace (Gal. 4:21–31). And so a Muslim is made *a spiritual child of Isaac* when the gospel is believed!

The command to sacrifice Isaac was God's way of teaching His people that the blessing of Abraham and the continuity of his seed was to be at a spiritual level, as being ones raised from the dead. His seed is by regeneration (new birth) not by procreation. God wants to transition us from the flesh into the spirit, from the natural into the resurrection realm. Abraham really did give up on Isaac and opened his heart to the resurrection realm of God. His tie to Isaac was forever spiritual from this day on. This 'parable' is one of the most powerful lessons God can teach us. God's work is always in the realm of resurrection — after dying to the natural. All of Abraham's posterity who does not likewise go through this test is counted as a son of haste, with Hagar for a mother.

God is the One, who claims total responsibility for the continuation of Isaac's seed, for only God can raise the dead. What begins in the spirit will often sink to being propped up by the flesh (Gal. 3:3). God's approval yesterday, does not guarantee His affirmation today. We must move on in the Spirit without presumption.

One of the great promises given to Abraham on Mt. Moriah was that his descendants would be 'city-reachers' — those who take possession of the gates of cities! Here in Genesis 22, God prophesies of a day when cities would be taken for God. Strategies for reaching cities come from the blessing God gave to Abraham! When we lay down our agendas like Abraham had to lay down his son, we will see our cities reached by the power of God

(Matt. 16:18)! Giving up the 'Isaac' of ministry ambitions will lead
to the grace from heaven to take a city for God. We are to press
forward into God's grace until cities all over the world are given to
the worship of Jesus Christ — it is our destiny!

The remaining paragraph gives us the information of Nahor,
Abraham's brother, having eight sons (8 = new beginning). One of
these sons was Bethuel, the father of **Rebekah**. She will be of great
interest as the story of the **Spiritual Seed** unfolds....

ABRAHAM POSSESSES THE LAND (GEN. 23)

The bond of love between Abraham and Sarah is broken by death.
She dies at 127 years of age. She died in the land of Canaan where
she had lived as a foreigner for over 60 years. Her place of death
was Hebron ('fellowship'). Sarah died, but other women of faith
would follow.

Abraham sincerely lamented over the passing of his wife, the
mother of Isaac. He sat down by her corpse and wept over her, paying
tribute to her life of faith with his tears (Heb. 11:13). Abraham
rises (in faith) after the time of mourning and asks for a burial plot
from the Hittites. This burial in the land of Canaan signaled there
was no turning back for Abraham and his descendants. The future
of this 'mighty prince' would now be in Canaan. Securing land was
important for this statement to be made.

It is quite interesting to see the negotiations of the burial place,
the price to be paid, and the humility of Abraham. Both Ephon's
field and the cave at Machpelah ('double-cave') were deeded over
to Abraham after the purchase price was agreed upon (about 4.5
kilograms of silver). Abraham now owned the landed lawfully.
Although God had promised it, he still paid a price to possess it.
His heart would now be bound to the land. We cannot help but
notice Abraham's honesty in these matters. All was 'above board'
and proper with the Hittites (I Thess. 4:12).

It is worth noting that a burial plot became the first piece of land Abraham possessed in Canaan. To walk into our inheritance we must die daily. Death will be a reminder to us ... His death for us, and our dying to our own darkness. The cave was at the **"end of the field."** We need to take an early end to our own life that we might discover the end of the Lord.

Our hearts must be turned to the God of resurrection or all our hopes are vain in the face of our ancient foe, death. The hope of the gospel sets before us a glorious immortality that lives beyond our tombs. In the morning of resurrection we will see the value of a life of faith. It is clear that Abraham had his eyes on resurrection. He had faith that someday Messiah would come and be raised from the dead. The purchase of the cave was an act of faith and anticipation (Matt.27:52–53). Abraham cared more for the sepulcher than for his tent ... his eyes were on the expectation of resurrection.

Abraham's intention in purchasing the cave of Machpelah was not only to bury Sarah there, but also to bury him. The word Machpelah means *'double'* or *'doubling.'* Everyone who buried in this cave would be as one of a couple — Abraham and Sarah, Isaac and Rebekah, Jacob and Leah (Gen.23:19, 25:9, 49:29–32, 50:13). Faith was strong and deep within Abraham, faith in the resurrection to come. Death for the patriarchs was a gateway into the resurrection. This cave was more like a 'bedroom' to rest, rather than a tomb. The God of Abraham, Isaac, and Jacob, is not a God of the dead, but of the living (Matt.21:32). He is our God!

Chapter Nine

GIFTS FOR THE BRIDE
"HE WILL SEND HIS ANGEL BEFORE YOU."

I saac was now 40 years old. Culturally, it was expected that he would be married by the age of 30. Isaac was overdue for a wife! Before Abraham died, he wanted to see his son marry and give him grandsons — for they would be the 'seed' of promise. Blessings would await his grandchildren, for God had made Abraham rich. The burden on this old man's heart was that Isaac would marry a woman from their family line. One who would preserve the purity of their lineage. He saw that the Canaanites were descending into great wickedness. Isaac must marry one of his kindred.

The chief servant of the household (Eliezar) was commissioned to go and look for a bride. With unquestioned loyalty he was given the responsibility of finding the appropriate spouse for this son of promise. He was with Abraham from the beginning and was responsible for everything that Abraham owned. He must go to a far country, across the wilderness and find a worthy bride for Isaac.

Clearly, we see a picture of the Father releasing the Holy Spirit to seek out a Bride for His Son, Jesus Christ. It is the Father that brings the Bride to Jesus as His love gift to the Son (John 17:24). In picture form, the details of this chapter point us to the heavenly scene of gathering a Bridal-partner for Jesus from the nations of the earth. The Church is the Bride, the Lamb's wife (Rev. 21:9). His ministers are *"friends of the Bridegroom"* who are sent to awaken bridal love in the nations as they persuade souls to espouse their heart to Him (John 3:29, Matt. 9:15, & II Cor. 11:2).

Only the trusted Servant, the Holy Spirit, is capable of drawing hearts to the Son, imparting endless love for Him. The name Eliezer means 'the God of help' or 'the God of comfort.' Is not the Holy Spirit our Helper, the Comforter (II Cor. 1:3)?

"The servant asked him, "What if the woman is unwilling to come back with me to this land?" The servant, bound by oath to do as Abraham commanded, had placed his hands in the private parts of the aged patriarch and bound himself by oath. The Holy Spirit is under "oath" to bring back a Bride to the Lord Jesus! There must be a willing bride for the heavenly Isaac. She will be willing to leave all to follow this Prince. She will be willing to follow the Holy Spirit as He leads us back to **"this land."**

Should Abraham die before he saw the wedding, this oath would still be in force. Under no conditions was the servant to take Isaac into the land to search for a bride, the bride must be willing to come and dwell in the place of promise. Abraham prophesies that the Lord's angel would go with him in search for Isaac's partner. The success of this mission would be found in Divine intervention. Angels will assist in bringing in the Bride! The wife of Isaac must be from his own people — so the Bride of Christ must be of **His** own family, born from above. He must have an equal yoke partner to share His throne. This Bride will be the sharer of all the Son's dignity and glory (John 17:22–23). The **Seed** of Isaac and his Bride will bless all the nations of the earth. They possess everything together!

Eliezer takes with him 10 camels loaded with gifts for the bride. One camel for himself and 9 **For The Bride**. There are 9 gifts of the Holy Spirit (I Cor.12:8–10), and 9 fruits of the Holy Spirit (Gal. 5:22–23). The Holy Spirit comes to us bearing gifts for the Bride. He decked her with gold (the Divine Nature) and talked about Isaac all the way home (Gen. 24:65). This is a picture of the Holy Spirit placing upon us the gold of the righteousness of Christ and revealing how wonderful our Prince truly is (John 16:13–15)!

The servant went to a well of water just outside the city. The Bride would be the woman at the well! After a wearying journey, the servant of Abraham had his camels kneel as he waited by the well at **"evening"** (at the end of the age a Bridal company will come forth). Then he prayed for the God of Abraham to send the woman He had chosen to be the bride of Isaac. He asked for a very specific sign that would show the true nature of the bride-to-be....

Would she be willing to give 10 thirsty camels water from the well? The woman's willingness to serve water showed that she had a true servant-spirit. What work to draw water for these thirsty camels! She would have to lower her bucket down the well **Many** times, for one camel can drink 20 gallons ... all for a stranger. It was evening. It would be dark after she was done. This would be an exceptional woman to do something like this ... may *we* become a servant bride!

"Before he had finished praying, Rebekah came out with the jar on her shoulder." No sooner did Eliezer pray these things that Rebekah came to draw water from the well. Humbly this woman gave herself to the stranger, the needy. She would be the one that was fit to be the bride of Isaac. She did exactly what Eliezer prayed she would do. This one act of service qualified Rebekah to be Isaac's bride and to be brought into the line of Christ and His inheritance. We do not realize how one act of humble service will affect the world and bring promotion to our own life (Matt. 10:42).

Can you imagine this scene? He had only asked for a little drink and she volunteers to offer a lot. She has an extravagant spirit. With enthusiasm Rebekah is willingly serving a stranger at great cost to her. That bucket had to be heavy! **"So she *quickly* emptied her jar into the trough, *ran* back to the well to draw *more* water, and drew enough for *all* his camels."** The Lord will find His most faithful servants in these last days doing menial tasks with joy; hidden from the eyes of others. Are you faithful to God in serving with enthusiasm in the small things? When the true bridal spirit comes forth in us, we will love to serve like Jesus loves to serve.

The name **Rebekah** means, 'captivating beauty' or 'grace that enraptures.' She was a beautiful maiden who was willing to get dirty for God! You are His Bride beautiful. A willing spirit makes us beautiful to Him as He adorns us in grace. Just as Rebekah was **"a virgin,"** You have been washed clean before God regardless of what you have been saved from. This must now be your identity.

Upon inquiry, Eliezer found that she was a near relative to his master (Isaac's second cousin) and that she came from a family of considerable stature. This was going to be one marriage made in heaven! He gave her a gold nose ring and two gold bracelets. These are tokens of love for the Bride. This was not a payment for services rendered — but a recognition of the bride-to-be!

Can you believe Rebekah took Eliezer and his camels home for the night? There was room in her inn for the Master's Servant. This invitation brought Eliezer to his knees in worship. He saw that the God of Abraham had gone before him and answered his prayer. The girl ran ahead and prepared the household for their visitor while Eliezer had church! She has been drawn by grace and is now "running" after Him (Song of Songs 1:4).

What energy Rebekah had! After filling over 100 buckets of water she now **Runs** home to tell her household what had taken place. Rebekah's brother, Laban, saw her running home with all this gold on and knew something good was up (Prov. 18:16). So he went to find Eliezer and bring him home. Eliezer was still worshipping at the well! **"Come, you who are blessed by the Lord,"** he said. **"Why are you standing out here? I have prepared the house and a place for the camels."** How we need to open our hearts prepare for God's Spirit to fill our 'house.'

"So the man went to the house and the camels were unloaded...." Don't you want the Holy Spirit to 'unload' His gifts in your church (house)? Eliezer was so caught up in this moment that he refused to eat until he could explain his purpose in being there. It was the custom of the Middle East to always eat first and talk business later when entertaining guests. But Eliezar was focused on his mission. As a faithful servant, he told them all about Abraham, his wealth, and about his son, Isaac. How the Holy Spirit loves to brag on the magnificence of Jesus! Then, he told them of the miracle at the well and how God answered his prayer. Then he asks the family to surrender Rebekah to become the bride of Isaac. What would they say? What would Rebekah say?

"This is from the Lord." So many times we think the events of our life are happenstance, but they may be a 'Divine setup' to release the next phase of destiny in our lives. **"Here is Rebekah; take her and go, and let her become the wife of your master's son, as the Lord has directed."** They understood the timing was supernatural. They could not say no to the Lord.

When Abraham's servant heard this, he bowed down in worship and brought out even more gifts for the bride. Gold and silver jewelry, fine clothing and costly gifts — for the whole family!

The next day, the family begged Eliezer to wait ten more days as they said their farewells to Rebecca. This would be hard to say good bye to one so loved. Eliezer pressed his plea to go. Today is the day to say 'Yes' to God. He did not want to keep his master waiting that long. Finally, they decided to ask Rebekah what she thought. Her reply? **"I will go."** Among the Hebrews there can be no valid betrothal unless the bride freely consents. This then is the engagement of Rebekah to Isaac.

So they sent her off with her nurse (personal servant) with this blessing: **"Our sister, may you increase to thousands upon thousands; may your offspring possess the gates of their enemies."** Rebekah's household prophesied a blessing over her and her seed. Destiny hung over them that moment as the Spirit of Prophecy fell. The prophetic blessing is this: The 'seed' of Rebekah received the same blessing as the 'seed' of Abraham — they would possess the gates of their enemies. **Possess** not just knock down. They would take cities! They would possess the places once held by God's enemies.

This is a prophetic promise of a coming anointing that would reach cities. This city-reaching power comes when God's people walk with a 'Rebekah spirit.' We must become Rebekah's 'spiritual seed,' so that we may enter into the gate-taking anointing for our cities. Notice the qualities of this woman, a type of the church:

➤ She was a virgin with a servant-spirit.

➤ She was submitted to her household (church).

➤ She saw the purpose of God, with an ear for Divine things.

➤ She was willing to sacrifice loved ones to reach her destiny.

➤ She was prepared to walk an unknown path with God.

➤ She was blessed by her household.

➤ She was willing to follow Eliezer (Holy Spirit)

➤ She is decked with silver (redemption) & gold (Divine Nature).

➤ She followed Eliezer until she saw Isaac.

➤ She covered herself (humility) with a veil before Isaac.

"So the servant *took* Rebekah and left." She is taken away by the Spirit to go through the wilderness and meet her Bridegroom face to face! Have you been "taken"? Isaac had been dwelling at the well of water called **"Beer Lahai Roi"** which means, the Well of the Living One who Sees Me." Isaac lived his days in the revelation that God was watching over him. His real contentment was found in the revelation of the love of God who always watched over him. But the day came that he could sit still no longer — he had to go out and look for her to come. He went on a prayer-walk for his bride!

When Rebekah saw **Him**, she 'fell' (literal Hebrew) off her camel and went to meet him. In a token of modesty and humility, Rebekah veils herself as she meets her fiancé. Those who are espoused to Christ must likewise be quick to humble themselves before the Prince & King. It was the sight of her bridegroom that brought this response to Rebekah. She was not ashamed or embarrassed, she was saying, 'You are greater than I.'

Isaac was an affectionate son, holding the loss of his mother for these three years until comforted by Rebekah. Isaac was an affectionate husband; **"he loved her."** The heavenly Isaac loved His mother, even on the cross — and O how He loves His Bride! The joy He longed for is now in His arms.….

Chapter Ten

JACOB & ESAU
"TWO NATIONS ARE IN YOUR WOMB."

After the marriage of Isaac, we read of Abraham's second marriage. **Keturah** bore him six sons when he was nearly 140 years old. It is believed that Keturah was the most prominent of his maidservants.[19]

Isaac becomes the heir of all things (Heb.1:2) which would include heir of the promises given to him by God. The land would belong to Isaac, with portions of his estate given to his sons, both to Ishmael and to the six sons of Keturah. This was done while Abraham still lived. It is unfortunate that in our culture today it is done afterwards, when it cannot be seen or guided by a wiser hand. These sons were sent away to lands distant from Isaac, thus preserving the promise of inheritance to the beloved son of Abraham and Sarah.

Living at least another 35 years after the marriage of Isaac and Rebekah, we hear no more about supernatural experiences or encounters with the Lord. There are always seasons when we walk by faith, without clear visions or dreams to guide us. The Word of the Lord someday will be in us, not just invading our dreams.

For nearly 100 years Abraham and his family lived in Canaan. The appointed hour came; he died at 175. He died at a ripe old age and was still full of life. Longing for a better place he left all behind for his eternal reward. He finished his course in faith and was **"gathered to his people"** in the afterlife.

Death gathers us to our people. Those that are our people while we live will be our people after we die. His sons, Ishmael and Isaac buried him, laying their differences aside in their common sorrow; burying him in the same cave where Sarah was buried.

The Scripture indicates that the favor of God was passed on to Isaac. Clearly, his life was blessed and anointed as the son of promise. He walked in the knowledge that God, the Living One, would never leave him. He was born by supernatural power; he was figuratively raised from the dead on Mt. Moriah, and now he walked into the realm of favor given by the promises of God to his father Abraham. Isaac was a man of the well (25:11, 26:18–25).

ISHMAEL AND ISAAC (25:12–23)

Ishmael's 12 sons (tribal leaders) are listed as those who peopled the land of Arabia. Isaac was 40 when he married Rebekah who was barren until Isaac prayed for her. Like his father, Isaac was an intercessor.

Rebekah became pregnant[20] with twins who **"jostled each other within her."** Curious, she asked why this was happening, the Lord answered her (audibly?) saying, **"Two nations are in your womb, and two peoples from within you will be separated; one will be stronger than the other..."** (v.23). Rebekah received this prophecy before the twins were born (Rom. 9:10–13). They had waited 20 years before the miracle of birth took place (v.26). The spiritual seed continues by the miracle power of God.

The struggle within the womb was quite intense. Their conflict was painful even before they were born. Her two sons were destined to be founders of great tribes. With an ongoing conflict, the eldest would become a servant to the younger. By sovereign choice God chose Jacob, the youngest, to receive the blessing. Rebekah, no doubt, remembered this promise in showing favor to Jacob.

"And the older will serve the younger." Esau and Jacob represented two nations within her womb (flesh and Spirit — Gal. 5:17). These are two types of people that must be separated. The elder would serve the younger (flesh must serve spirit, for spirit is stronger).

The principle of the second chosen over the first is illustrated many times in Scripture (i.e. Cain & Abel, Ishmael & Isaac, Manasseh & Ephraim). This is explained in I Cor. 15:46.... First the natural, then the spiritual (Adam & the Second Adam).

Can you imagine what would happen in the church today if the "older" would serve the "younger"? We must always make a way for the new thing God desires to do and for the new generation that God desires to bless. How often do we hear a church leader say to the young, 'Come and serve my vision.' Yet what would happen if a new breed of leadership arose to say, 'Come, you who are favored of the Lord — we will bless you and help you fulfill your vision.' A generational transfer must take place for the church to take the fullness of her inheritance.

ESAU AND JACOB (25:24–34)

The parents observed the details of their birth and named them accordingly. Esau, the firstborn, was hairy (Esau = 'hairy or shaggy'). His appearance was more like an animal of the field than a normal baby. His skin color was quite red, and was nicknamed Edom ('red').

The second child was born grasping the heel of his older brother and was named Jacob ('heel-grabber, supplanter' or 'to trip up'), which showed he was in essence, struggling for the best starting position. He wanted to be first! Jacob is a man that schemes and manipulates. He deceives to get his own way. Their names pointed to their destinies. This is the story of the birth of Israel (Jacob) and how God in grace chose the 'heel-grabber' to be the carrier of the promise to the nations. God elects to use the things that are weak and despised to confound the mighty (I Cor. 1:26–27).

"Jacob was a quiet man staying among the tents." Loved by his mother, Jacob was a homebody. Esau, on the other hand, was an outdoorsman and a skilled hunter. Like Nimrod, Esau was a man of the world who gained advantage through cunning craftiness. This made quite a household for Isaac and Rebekah! Esau knew how to please his father and won his heart by providing wild game to eat. Jacob knew how to please his mother and simply helped her in the house (tent) wherever he could. Rebekah preferred Jacob, for she remembered the word of the Lord given to her concerning him. This coveted birthright had four elements:

1 Until the establishing of the Aaronic priesthood it was the one with the birthright who was the head of the family and would exercise the priestly rights.

2 This birthright would be the lineage through which the Messiah, the Satan-bruiser (Gen. 3:15) would come.

3 The covenant blessings that God gave to Abraham would be passed on to the one possessing the birthright (Gen. 12:3).

4 A double portion of the father's goods (Deut. 21:17). Something to be desired and esteemed, the birthright would be one of the highest privileges given by God. Esau was in line to receive it.

Esau sold the privileges of the birthright as firstborn, to his younger brother, Jacob. The price? A good meal? More than that.... According to the Rabbi's, it was the duty of the firstborn to cook a meal of **Red** stew on a certain day of the year and place it on the grave of Abraham while the firstborn fasted. However, Esau, instead of performing this duty, was off hunting while Jacob did what the firstborn was responsible for. Esau's appetite became his master. Unable to wait for another meal, he insisted on eating the customary red stew reserved for honoring Father Abraham. (*"Jewish Encyclopedia, Esau"*).

With unchecked natural desires, Esau became filled with only one thought — filling his stomach. He was simply a man of the flesh, one who lived to gratify his natural desires. To satisfy his cravings, he gave up the honored privileges of the double portion.

What a sad picture of you and I when we say 'yes' to sin. The flesh is to be given over to crucifixion. Everything in us must give way to the increase of Jesus in our inner man. All of self will be taken away. Rather than let the flesh die Esau chose to live without the blessing. We are like the thief 'Barabbas' who wanted to be set free from the cross. Jesus would not come down from His cross. We must embrace the cross as deeply as He did.

Jacob coveted what Esau despised. He had an eye toward the spiritual blessings that would come to the one blessed of the father. Esau despised the birthright. He did not value the treasures of heaven that would be his. He only saw what was seen in the flesh. Godless Esau is a warning to all who seek to possess their spiritual inheritance (Heb.12:16–17). Esau exchanged one morsel of meat, one bowl of soup, for the princely privileges. He lived to regret it, though tears and remorse could never restore what he gave up. Gratifying sensual desires has eternal consequences (Phil.3:17–19).

Esau was mastered by the fragrance of a pot of stew, Samson by the charms of a Philistine girl, and Peter by the question of a maiden. There is no strength apart from the Strong Son of God! We do not understand human nature. We cannot pray for an hour, yet we think we have yielded our life fully to Christ. We cannot speak to one person on the street, yet we believe we could speak or preach behind a pulpit. Believers today read this story of Jacob and Esau and cannot understand how Esau could be so consumed with his hunger that he traded his birthright for this red stew. Yet just as easily we trade our privileges in God for the things of this world.

If we could have been there with Esau we would have put our hand on his shoulder and looked him in the eye with words like: 'Are you sure you want to do this Esau? Is it wise to give it all away for a momentary pleasure?' Now is the time to ask the *Esau that lives in you* these same questions. Your spiritual birthrights must be treasured and held dear — you are a child of God, destined to be like Christ. Your birthright is to stand side by side with Jesus Christ in His glory. He has given you the right to be more than conquerors over all the power of your enemies. We do not have to yield to sin.

Although Jacob was no match for his burly brother in physical strength, he made up for it in cunning craftiness. His scheme paid off; Jacob stole the birthright! After the meal, Esau carelessly got up and went away — not realizing what a grave mistake he made. He made no attempt to revoke the transaction. He gave to Jacob the birthright.

THE GOD OF ABRAHAM, ISAAC, AND JACOB[21]

The way in which God dealt with these three men, reveals what God wants to do with man. Abraham discovered Jehovah as the God of Promise. Isaac found Him to be the God of Miracles. Jacob learned that Jehovah is the God of Transformation. First, God gives us the promise. But the promise requires a miracle to perform it. This 'miracle-promise' releases true transformation within the heart of man. This is the revelation of the God of Abraham, Isaac, and Jacob.

Abraham is the father ... the starting point of recovery. This former idolater was given incredible promises of the glory and blessing of God. The call of God to Abram (Abraham) was to **Come Out** and be separated unto God. Abraham learned that God was the *Father*. In the same way, God must be to you, The God of Abraham. Wherever Abraham went, he made an *altar*.

Isaac is the Son and heir of all things. Born into wealth, he had nothing that was not given to him. He blessed his sons like Abraham did and was finally buried in the tomb bought by his father. Isaac received the blessings of miracle power and saw that everything the *Son* has is from the Father. In the same way, you must know God as the God of Isaac. Wherever Isaac went he dug a *well*.

Jacob was a man who learned the discipline of death to the flesh. He faced his fallen nature all through his days until he leaned upon God. Jacob was a fighter from birth. He was a man who could deceive anyone — his brother, his father, his uncle. Jacob must learn the ways of the *Spirit* and be transformed. In the same way, you must encounter God as the God of Jacob. Wherever Jacob dwelt he pitched a *tent*. What these three patriarchs went through **Together** reveals what the Lord will do in every royal believer today (I Cor. 10:11). When He becomes to the Church the God of Abraham, Isaac, and Jacob; He will have a people on the earth for Himself. As the foundations of the nation of Israel; Abraham, Isaac, and Jacob are also the foundation of all that God plans to do in the human soul.

---

[19] Keturah is called Abraham's concubine in I Chronicles 1:32. Her name signifies 'incense,' or 'perfume.' She brought sweetness into the life of Abraham.

[20] During their 20-year wait for children, there is no mention that Isaac fathered children with his handmaiden, as his father Abraham did. Isaac loved Rebekah and was patient and prayerful until the miracle happened.

[21] See Matthew 22:32.

Chapter Eleven

THE ALTAR, TENT, & WELL
"THE LORD APPEARED TO ISAAC..."

This is the only chapter of Genesis devoted exclusively to Isaac. With famine facing him in Canaan, Isaac lived at Gerar, a Philistine city with a king named Abimelech. God appears to Isaac and instructs him not to go down to Egypt; he was to remain in the land. God can provide food for us even in a land of famine. Isaac is reassured that all the land given to Abraham would be his. Destiny must be fulfilled. Isaac would not die. The Lord renews His Covenant with Abraham and passed the promises on to Isaac.

Father and son both fell into the same sin. Abraham and Isaac lied about their wives, convincing the pagans that they were merely their sisters. This passage makes it clear that both the blessing of the fathers and the sin of the fathers are passed on to the next generation. God rescued Isaac from a blunder that would have had major consequences. Isaac's "seed" was to be multiplied like the stars of the heavens. The spiritual seed of Isaac would be those true Israelites that could receive everything from their Father. Isaac is a picture of sonship. Isaac's seed will be sons and daughters who walk in the fullness of their inheritance by faith.

100-FOLD INCREASE

"Isaac planted crops in that land and the same year reaped a hundredfold, because the *Lord* blessed him." God's blessing was upon Isaac, even in the border city of Gerar ('lodging place'). He sowed his seed and reaped a bountiful harvest; a hundred fold blessing from God! Isaac was blessed because he did not hoard the seed. He sowed on the enemy's land and reaped a great harvest during a time of famine (Deut. 28:1–13, Isaiah 65:13, Ps. 37:19). God does bless His people! Isaac was envied by the Philistines and soon expelled from their land.

Isaac reopened ancient wells. God's **Spiritual Seed** will always be those who respect the wisdom of the elders but will go on to dig their own wells. The jealous Philistines filled Isaac's well with dirt. No matter where Isaac dug and no matter how often the Philistines threw dirt in his well, Isaac would open them back up again!

This is what we must do when the enemy wants to clog our spiritual life and keep us from springing up in fresh power. Go back and clean out the old well! Wells speak of a source of satisfaction, a fountain. When there is no satisfaction, no water; it is time to dig deeper! Even in the lowest valley, there is refreshment waiting for those who will dig for it!

The one who dug a well in those days became the owner of that well. It was not a community source but a private source of supply. There will always be those who don't want a flow of fresh revelation in your life (Matt. 23:13). Some want us perpetually dependent on them for truth. God will always help you to dig your own well. The word used here for **"fresh water"** can be translated 'springing water' — a well to refresh and reveal new truths....

Isaac refused to fight back. The Philistines quarreled with Isaac over the first and second well they dug. **Esek** means 'strife, argument' and **Sitnah** means 'hostility, contention.' Refusing to be turned aside with vain strife (I Tim. 1:4), Isaac moved on and dug a third well called **Rehoboth**, 'a broad place, enlargement, room enough.' God's **Spiritual Seed** will not be given to strife and contention. We must choose peace over winning an argument.

In **Beersheba**, God dug a well in Isaac. The strife with others had taken toll on Isaac. It was time for a fresh encounter with God. When others were jealous, continually harassing him, faithful Isaac was visited by God. In this difficult place, Isaac built an altar of worship, pitched his tent, and dug a well. This will always accompany God's **Spiritual Seed** — the *altar*, the *tent*, and the *well*. Even in the midst of our enemies, we can meet God at the personal altar of worship. The tent pictured the pilgrim heart of Isaac — always ready to move on at the call of God. The Lord truly smiled on what Isaac had done in forgiving his enemies, for the same day he made this covenant with Abimelech, his servants brought him the news of a fresh well of water they found. Since Isaac was silent over the offense of losing wells, God honored him with a new one. Beersheba became the place of renewed covenant with God and man (Beersheba = 'seven, complete, fulfillment, oath, covenant').

PULLING THE WOOL OVER DAD'S EYES (GEN. 25)

The chapter opens with the blindness of Isaac. Isaac did not deal with Esau concerning his Canaanite wives. He loved Esau's wild game more than he loved Esau. Isaac, approaching his time of death, knew that he must impart the blessing he received from Abraham. Ignoring the word that the elder would serve the younger, he sought to release this blessing to Esau. Overhearing his instructions to Esau to prepare his meal, Rebekah told Jacob to hurry off and fix the meal before Esau returned from hunting.

The promise of the Messiah and the land of Canaan was a great trust, first given to Abraham, passed on to Isaac — and now ready to be given to Isaac's son. What power there was in Isaac's blessing! The course of human history would be changed by the outcome … would Esau receive it, or Jacob? It seemed right for the firstborn, Esau, to inherit the blessing. Nevertheless, the Lord used even Jacob's trickery to bring upon him the desired blessing. How gracious is God!

Rebekah thought she was pursuing the best course, for she remembered the promise of the elder serving the younger. She could not stand to see Esau, who had broken her heart by taking foreign wives, be blessed. This entire episode is a testimony to the conniving nature of man and the overriding purposes of God that cannot be thwarted by our sin. This family was a mess. None of them did what was right or noble in God's sight — yet His purpose was fulfilled. Isn't that the story of all our lives? We compete for the blessing, we trick and deceive others, we choose the flesh over the Spirit, and we think God needs our help to pull it off! See Job 12:16

Isaac was deceived by his senses; smell, taste, and feel. How often does this happen to you? We must become those who walk in the Spirit and have crucified the flesh with its desires. Jacob lied. He told his father that he was Esau. Then he lied again when his father asked if it was really Esau. Once more he lied in saying that God provided the wild game for him — sin multiplies in the heart of a deceiver.

How corrupt is the heart of man! How often we feel God needs our help. This 'Jacob' life is within us all. Before God breaks us, we will always resort to our cleverness to attain the blessing. We speak the language of a saint but do the work of a sinner. We must be those who clothe ourselves in our **Elder Brother's Garments** to receive the blessing of our Father!

We see this man Jacob about the 'pull the wool over the eyes' of his father. Jacob sets the meal before his father and waits until dinner is done — he wants the blessing! Isaac praises his son and bestows the coveted blessing upon the head of the wrong one. What an intriguing picture … God is about to bless Jacob … Isaac wants the blessing to go to Esau…. Jacob deceives his father into thinking he is Esau … and God's purpose is fulfilled. O, the depth of the riches and knowledge of God (Rom. 11:33–36)! What looked like a mistake and a fraud actually fulfilled the purposes of heaven.

If it is true in this account, it is true in your life. Everything works into the flow of heaven when we love God and are called according to His purpose (Rom. 8:28). Never underestimate the power of God to turn your failures into fruitfulness, if you keep loving Him!

Jacob is blessed with three things … riches, power, and prevailing grace. Heaven and earth will work together to make him rich; the dew of heaven and the fatness of the earth. The power of dominion will be his, especially over his brethren. Prevailing grace will shield him. Curses coming to those who curse him; and blessings to those who bless him. God will be a Friend to all his friends; an Enemy to all Jacob's enemies. These are the blessings of the Father to every **Spiritual Seed** of Abraham, Isaac, and Jacob.

Can you see these three blessings flowing onto and out from the Messiah, our Lord Jesus? The **Blessing** really belongs to Him and to those He shares it with. All the treasures of heaven and earth belong to Him. He alone has all dominion over the kingdoms of this world. Jesus, the Messiah King is honored and blessed by the Father; and woe to those who seek to curse Him! He is the **Top Branch** of the Lord. He has the stars and the scepter in His hand (Num. 24:19). This **Branch-Man** is on the earth in His corporate Body with the authority and blessing of heaven. Though we may be deceivers like Jacob, the purpose of the Lord will stand.

Esau now seeks the blessing, but it is too late. No man could have been more disappointed in life than Esau. With trembling and bitter tears he sought the blessing, but it would not be his (Heb. 12:17). This is always the case. We esteem too lightly the blessings of God, only years later to be filled with remorse over letting them slip (Heb. 2:1). Even though Jacob obtained it fraudulently, Isaac confirms to Esau that it now belongs to Jacob (Rom. 9:16). Esau still asked if Isaac only had one blessing to give; couldn't he also speak a blessing over Esau? Esau received a second-rate blessing, as one separated from the birthright. The spirit of prophecy moved Isaac as he spoke over his son....

Esau would be given all the provisions he would need in life. Notice that Isaac reverses the order — the fatness of the earth is given first, for Esau would be a man with his heart attached to the world. Esau would serve, but he would not starve. He would live by the 'sword-principle;' always retaliating, unable to forgive. How many in the church today has enough of God to get by, but live with unresolved anger and unforgiveness like Esau?

After much striving, Esau would break the yoke of bondage. This was fulfilled in a later generation with the Edomites (II Kings 8:20–22). Nowhere in Scripture do we see the Israelites under bondage to the Edomites. Esau would serve the younger.

Jacob was blessed with a kiss from his father; Esau was not. All of this caused Esau to hate his brother. Following in the way of Cain, he made an inner vow to murder his brother as soon as his father died. Such is the heart of man. Jealousy turns to hatred, hatred to murder; all because our brother received a blessing that we did not.

What Esau desired was to kill Jacob so that he would not enjoy any of the blessings prophesied over him. How often in the church does this spirit work to incite jealousy over those who have been blessed by our Father. Forgetting that they are brothers, we become persecutors of the favored ones.

The 'Faith Chapter' gives us a remarkable insight into this account. God commends Isaac in Hebrews 11:20 — *"By **Faith** Isaac blessed Jacob and Esau in regard to their future."* At first glance, it does not appear to be an act of faith, but a blunder for Isaac to bless Jacob instead of Esau. But God called it **Faith** ... What does this mean? *Isaac refused to change what he had done.* In faith, Isaac blessed Jacob, even though he thought it was Esau; and when he discovered he had been tricked, he stuck to his guns — **"indeed, he shall be blessed!"**

Isaac blessed his sons in faith, for he knew the authority that God had given him. Isaac, refusing to reverse the blessing, was demonstrating great faith. It proved that Isaac realized that the **Spiritual Seed** could not continue on an earthly level, but a spiritual one. Though he did not deserve it, Isaac let the blessing stand with Jacob.

All of this was contrary to Isaac's natural inclination. Instead of doubt or unbelief, he acted by faith. It is the nature of faith to give priority to God's will rather than our own. This is exactly what Abraham had to do with Isaac. Now Isaac had to give up Esau and his opinion of how God was to accomplish His purposes.

Rebekah gives warning to Jacob and sends him away. This would be the last time she sees her son before she dies. Rebekah hoped that Jacob would remain out of sight long enough for the jealous rage of Esau to subside. Convincing Isaac that it would not be prudent for Jacob to marry a Canaanite woman, Jacob's parents send him to Laban; thus preserving his life. Jacob ran away like a refugee. Alone and afraid, God had Jacob right where He wanted him....

Chapter Twelve

THE JESUS STAIRWAY
"JACOB...HAD A DREAM...
HE SAW A STAIRWAY."

J acob now flees the anger of his brother to hide at his uncle Laban's house in Haran (Syria). Before he leaves, Isaac again speaks a blessing over the **Spiritual Seed**. The two great blessings of Abraham — a land of prosperity and a multitude of generations were passed from Isaac to Jacob. Jacob is probably 77 at this time.[22]

Esau went to Ishmael and took his daughter Mahalath to be his third wife (28:6–9). Both Ishmael and Esau picture those of the flesh life, for 'birds of a feather flock together.' Esau joined with a family God had rejected, all of this to please his parents, not God.

Jacob was now alone. You can almost imagine what filled his thoughts as he walked along with only his staff. Surely he must have thought about how wrong it was to deceive his father. He undoubtedly grieved over leaving his mother behind. Perhaps he wondered what kind of reception he would receive from Laban....

Whatever his thoughts, Jacob was at the end of himself as he journeyed from Beersheba toward Haran (Syria).

Sixty miles from Beersheba Jacob stumbled into **"a certain place"** — the place of God's purpose and design. This nothing-special-place was Haran, which means 'a dry or parched place.' Sometimes when you think you are in a dry place, you are really on your way to meet God. Maybe you are at that place right now....

Having walked for a number of days, he was weary and exhausted as night fell. In the twilight he sets up camp at Bethel. Some believe this was the ancient place where his grandfather, Abraham, years ago erected an altar to Yahweh (12:8). In his helpless, lonely condition, a new revelation would be given to Jacob. Stones for a pillow ... How hard a time it must have been in Jacob's life. With heaven as a canopy above and the cold ground beneath, Jacob falls asleep and dreams. He sees a vision of the Almighty and hears the words of God.

Jacob sees a stairway, a ladder reaching up to heaven. Upon this ladder, ascending and descending, were angels. God Himself was at the top of this angel — filled stairway speaking to him.

Jesus Christ is clearly the ladder that reaches from earth (His human nature) to heaven (His heavenly nature). Jesus spoke to Nathaniel using the same terminology — *"I tell you the truth, you shall see heaven open, and the angels of God ascending and descending upon the Son of Man. (John 1:51)"* Jacob received the glorious revelation that Jesus is the **Stairway** to heaven! By Him we climb and leave this lower life. It is when we see Him that the Father speaks to our hearts. All of God's favors come to us on this Jesus-Ladder. Jesus is the only valid entry into the spirit realm, the true way into the heavenlies.

The church ladders all fall short, never reaching the sky. But there is a ladder that does reach all the way and bridges the gap. That ladder is Christ. His wonderful deeds, His precious blood, His mighty resurrection have made the reach from earth to heaven. We now have a Ladder to climb. Through heaven's prayer ladder we ascend and descend with the glory upon us. Our life can be a "gate" to heaven. Every praying believer is climbing Jacob's ladder to touch the eternal and release it back to the earth.

This Jesus-Ladder was filled with angels ascending and descending. Who are these angels? Note the order: they ascended first. It does not say they were descending and ascending which would be true if they were the angels in heaven. If you ascend first, you are leaving earth to go to heaven. These angels are intercessors, *promise-claimers!* The Hebrew word translated angel is 'malak,' which can also be translated ambassador, deputy, messenger, or prophet. The Greek word used in the New Testament for angel is merely, 'angelos' or 'messenger.' They can refer to people or to angels. Paul wrote to the Galatians and told them they had welcomed him in their midst as if he were an *angel* of God (Gal. 4:14). In Revelation 2–3, John is instructed to write to the seven churches and to the seven "angels" of those churches. Those angels were messengers or pastors over those churches. Even Jesus, in His pre-incarnate form, appeared in the Old Testament as the Angel of the Lord.

In Genesis 18:2 three angels come to Abraham and are described as **"three men"** (Cp. Gen. 19:1). Angels are also seen as the end-time reapers (Matthew 24:31). God's messengers, will be sent as fiery flames of revival into all the earth. From the ministry of angels (messengers) the great harvest will be brought in. We are the angelic-ambassadors that ascend and descend upon the Jesus-Ladder![23]

This revelation repeated by our Lord to Nathaniel. Nathaniel had his eyes on the earth (*"Can any good thing come out of Nazareth"*) but Jesus told him his eyes would see heaven opened.

Listen to the words of St. Germanus of Constantinople[24] as he speaks of this 'ladder-climbing' … "The souls of Christians are called to assemble with the prophets, apostles, and hierarchs in order to recline with Abraham, Isaac, and Jacob at the mystical banquet of the Kingdom of Christ. Thereby having come into the unity of faith and communion of the Spirit through the dispensation of the One who died for us and is sitting at the right hand of the Father, we are no longer on earth but standing by the royal Throne of God in heaven, where Christ is, just as He Himself says: 'Righteous Father, sanctify in Your Name those whom You have me, so that where I am, they may be with Me."

End-time intercession must become an act of climbing the Jesus-Ladder. We go up to the heavens with our cries for intervention. Then we descend back to earth with the answer! Intercession is seeing heaven open and the messengers of God ascending and descending upon the Son of Man. Each rung on the ladder is a progressive revelation of Jesus and our inheritance in Him.

It is time to go up, holy angels! It is time to let your heart-cry ascend until the promise descends. We need answers to our prayers! We must ascend the Hill of the Lord, the Jesus-Ladder until He rains down His Spirit upon us. We **All** have access to the Father by one Spirit (Eph.2:18). His door is open and the stairway is available to **You**. Before you can climb, believe you are His angel, and believe that you can ascend. The answers you need are not on the earth — they are in the Throne Room — and heaven is closer than you think.

Hello angel ... Did you go to heaven today? Did you ascend and get the will of God for today? Did you bring it back and execute it? Are you on the stairway today? Climb that Jesus-Ladder and find the fulfillment of your covenant promises, just like Jacob did. God says, 'You have to come where I live to get what you need. You have access to the heavenlies. I left the door open and the lights on. Come up, you mighty angels and praise the Lord for His mighty works.' Answers to prayer will be found when we ascend with the request and return in faith with the promise fulfilled. This is the hidden way of the stairs, the hiding places on the mountainside (Song of Songs 2:14).

What would God tell Jacob? Would He scold him for being a crafty deceiver? Would He rebuke him for his lack of faith? Perhaps God will just strike him dead for all the rotten things he has done … No, He reveals Himself to Jacob as the One who will never leave or forsake Him. This is a revelation of grace — a stream of assurances washes over wayward Jacob! The Lord renews the ancient promises with Jacob. He is given the blessing that Abraham and Isaac possessed. Jacob's descendants would spread out and cover the land like the dust of the earth. The **Spiritual Seed** would continue through *Jacob!* His descendants would bring forth the "Offspring" which would bless the whole earth.

JACOB AWAKENS AND MAKES A VOW (28:16–22)

As Jacob stirs from his supernatural slumber, he awakens with the exclamation — **"Surely the Lord is in this place, and I was not aware of it."** How many times have we been led to a place we were not comfortable with, only to encounter the Lord? Have you said, looking back over your life — 'Surely the Lord really was in all I went through, and I didn't even know it!' We often meet with God and miss it. He is where we did not think He had been. There is not a place you could be and not have a Divine visit. Ordinary places can become holy places…

Jacob was afraid, convinced that he had stumbled into a dreadful place. He called it the **"house of God … the gate of heaven."** This is the first mention of God's house in the Scriptures. The house of God was filled with His presence, a gateway to heaven, a stairway with angels and revelation.

The more we see of God, the more awesome will be our view of Him. If the flesh is not dealt with, the House of God **Is** a dreadful place. Jacob had great respect for this place of Divine Encounter. He saw it as the House of the Lord, the residence of Divine Majesty — the Gateway to Heaven, where God and man meet. Today, the house of God, the gate to heaven could also be a description of the church, God's house. The Lord dwells among us as His people. We become a gateway for others to come to God, with power to loose them from their sins (John 20:23). What Jacob saw was also a prophetic picture of the church that would come — where angels would ascend and descend.

Jesus spoke of this house to Nathaniel, the one He saw under the fig tree. The powerful word to this guileless man was this: "You will see heaven opened and the angels of God ascending and descending upon the Son of Man. Jesus is the Stairway to the skies. All that is said of God's House is said of Jesus.[25]

A memorial was built by Jacob to remember this Gateway, using the stone he had placed under his head. The very Christ on whom we rest will become the House of God. He builds a **Pillar** from his **Pillow**. The church is described by Paul as the "pillar and foundation of the truth" (I Tim.3:15). Pouring oil on the stone he consecrates the pillar as a memorial to God (Lev.8:10–11). As the Stairway had its top in heaven, Jacob anoints the top of the pillar with oil.

God uses stones to build His House, living stones. Placing them together, and then anointing them with oil, God transforms the stones into precious stones, jewels that make up the Celestial City, the New Jerusalem. The House of God can be built on earth. Fallen man always has the thought of going to heaven, but God's desire is to come down to earth and mingle Himself with mankind.

There is a House that will be built that is fitted on the earth but reaches into the heavens … Jacob pouring oil upon the stones signifies the pouring out of the Triune God upon His people … until they become His Bethel, the House of God.

The Anointed Stone — a Stone covered with oil — is Jesus. He is the Chief Cornerstone, the stone David threw at Goliath, the Stone that came and conquered kingdoms in Daniel 2. He is the Stone upon which you may lay your head! Jacob gives a new name to the place of revelation. He called the place **Bethel**, though it used to be called **Luz**. Bethel means 'house of God' — Luz means 'separation.' When we separate ourselves from the world we can enter the house of God. Jacob had to be driven from the house of Isaac to discover the house of God. Revelation is imparted when we separate our heart for the Lord in first love devotion. As we leave the flesh, we enter His House. This is where God will talk with us (Hosea 12:4, Ps.27:4)!

The revelation of the 'House of God' is growing among God's people. Jacob had only two things ... A heap of stones and a revelation. This is always how God begins. From what looks like ruins God will build His House. God is working on that heap of stones to shape and fashion according to His will as we are being built together for a habitation of God in the Spirit. Lord, take us from a heap of stones into becoming the Family you desire, the House of God!

Jacob now vows to make God his God. The Lord had renewed His covenant with Jacob, now it is time for Jacob to vow to God. The 'if' here could also mean, 'Seeing that God will be with me ...' Jacob furthermore vows to give back to God a tenth (tithe) of all that God gives to him. The proof that you have made fresh covenant with God is your finances! If you are not committed to God in your finances, you are not committed to God. With food and clothing, Jacob will be content with his God (I Tim.6:8). As a man with little to his name, it is a statement of great faith. He is changed from a wanderer to a worshipper. Will you walk as part of this **Spiritual Seed** in like faith? Take the stones from the place you are in and make a pillar of worship out of them!

The Lord gave these promises to Jacob while he still was unbroken, unreliable, a deceiver. God was confident that Jacob would never get away from His hand. Our God is a confident, capable God who can subdue and conquer the most difficult of men. Our future blessing and usefulness depends on God's strength, not ours. When God brought Jacob back to Bethel twenty years later, he was changed. God will change you. It may take more than a year, more than two years, more than 10 or 20 — but your God will finish the work of changing you into the image of His Son. You will be His look-alike. You will carry the blessings of God to the next generation!

"Jacob saw Rachel daughter of Laban, his uncle ... he went over and rolled the stone away from the mouth of the well and watered his uncle's sheep. Then Jacob kissed Rachel and began to weep aloud." Genesis 29:10–11

---

[22] Along with the blessing came a command not to be unequally yoked with a Canaanite wife (II Cor.6:14).

[23] Is this Isaiah's ascending "Highway"? Isa.35:8–9, 57:14–15, 62:10

[24] St. Germanus of Constantinople, On the Divine Liturgy, trans. Paul Meyendorff (Crestwood, NY: St Vladimir's Seminary Press, 1984), p.101.

[25] John 1:51

Chapter Thirteen

JACOB, RACHEL ... AND LEAH
"JACOB WAS IN LOVE WITH RACHEL..."

A fter the vision of the Jesus-Stairway, Jacob resumes his journey to Haran. The Hebrew text reads, 'Jacob lifted up his feet.' He lifted his foot to climb the Jesus-Stairway! As he arrives in Paddan Aram he sees a well with three flocks of sheep around it. These flocks were watered when the stone is rolled away. Beloved, there are a 30-fold, 60-fold, and 100-fold people who are watered (given life) after the stone over Jesus' tomb was rolled away (Matt.13:23; 28:1–2).

God had brought Jacob to the very well where Laban and his daughters, Rachel and Leah, watered their flocks. Jacob witnesses the shepherds watering their flocks and asks where they are from and if they knew Laban. At that very moment, Rachel appears with a flock of sheep. What a Divine appointment. One look at her and Jacob was hooked! He ran over and helped move the stone from off the well (perhaps to make an impression on lovely Rachel!). He kisses his cousin Rachel (they were kissin' cousins!) and begins to weep as he explains how he is related to her. She quickly runs to Laban to tell them as the whole household hurries out to the well to meet Jacob. Jacob made a superb entry into Paddan Aram!

After a month of working for Laban, he is asked what he thinks his wages should be. Because of his intense love for Rachel, Jacob offers to work for seven years in exchange for her hand in marriage. That is true love! Seven years! To Jacob, it seemed but a few days because of the love he had for her. Love can make long, hard service short and easy. This is why the Scriptures speak of a "labor of love" (I Thess.1:2, Heb.6:10). In Hosea 12:12 we learn that Jacob tended sheep for those seven years in order to get the bride he loved. There is Another who has waited now 7,000 years (7 weeks) for His Bride that He dearly loves! What has He done now for these years? He tends His flock like a Shepherd (Isa.40:11).

For those seven years, God was teaching Jacob submission to the rights of the *firstborn*. It was not right to marry the younger before the firstborn! All that Jacob circumvented in stealing the blessing from Esau, he now must learn by serving another for seven years and learn the timing of God. After the seven years was over, Laban tricked Jacob by giving him **Leah**, not Rachel on his wedding night. Leah was weak-eyed and perhaps, homely. Rachel was lovely and winsome. He woke up the next morning with the wrong one! Leah's name means, *'weary, sluggish'* and Rachel's name means *'lamb.'* Jacob must now work another seven years if he wanted to marry Rachel!

Laban was much more than Jacob bargained for. He finally met his match. Laban's words were **"You are my own flesh and blood!"** This is truer than Jacob realized. Both Laban and Jacob were unbroken, selfish men who connived and bargained their way around every difficulty. Through Laban, Jacob got a taste of his own medicine. The Lord knows how to break a man and empty him of self. No one can truly enjoy God as we were meant to, until self has been broken. Over and over again, God will bring us to the end of our cleverness. Jacob had cheated his father and brother, now Laban cheats Jacob.

The Lord will always have a Laban prepared for His unbroken servants. God will make sure we are led into that environment that will expose the weakness of our character — and true transformation will result. An unbroken man will meet an unbroken man sent by God to expose unresolved issues of the heart. This was a Divine setup. In all, Jacob worked for Laban for twenty years. During that time Laban changed his wages 10 times!

Perhaps it would be wise when we are thrown together with people who are crafty, arrogant, and contentious — before we lament that we have to be around such people we should take a long look at our heart. It may be that some of the traits we despise in others lay hidden in us. Those very people may be the ones God seeks to use to discipline *us*.

LEAH & RACHEL'S CHILDREN (29:31–35)

Leah was the mother of the first four children of Jacob. Leah, who was less loved, was favored while Rachel was denied this blessing. God's ways are not our ways. The Lord **Saw** that Leah was not loved. Rachel wants children but is blessed with her husband's love. Leah wanted Jacob's heart but was given children. There is a mercy-chord in God's heart that the broken, poor, and unloved touch. God gives greater honor to the dishonored ones (I Cor. 12:24). It is the nature of God to be drawn to those who hurt. Jesus saw her pain, her loneliness, and her heartache. If she only understood how greatly the Lord loved her....

The names Leah gave to her sons were an expression of her desires for her husband. She promised herself that the children she bore would turn his heart toward her. If the Lord opened her womb, surely He would open Jacob's heart. Leah's definition of fulfillment would only come through Jacob's love.[26] Envy is often rooted in a struggle to gain identity. With Leah and Rachel, there was an obvious competition to be **The** one who had Jacob's heart. So Leah called her first-born, Reuben, 'See! A son!' The Hebrew name Reuben also sounds like in Hebrew 'He has seen my misery.' Apparently, the birth of Reuben did not bring Leah any closer to Jacob's heart....

The second was named, Simeon, 'he hears,' which gives testimony to the grace of God in her life. Yet Jacob still loved Rachel more than Leah. Her third son was named Levi,[27] which means 'joined', in hopes that Jacob would become emotionally joined to her. Over the years of struggling with the pain of being unloved, Leah opens her heart to the Lord and grace touches her. God was tenderly wooing her to Himself through the disappointment of her marriage.

At last, she gives birth to her fourth son and resolves to praise the Lord no matter what. Leah has now become a worshipper of the Almighty. Leah found her fulfillment in God. She names her son Judah ('praise') and declares, 'This time I will praise the Lord!' This son became the father of the tribe of Judah, through whom Jesus was born after the flesh. Leah, not Rachel becomes the mother of Judah and ancestor of Jesus ... Now that the *Lion of Judah* has come, we too can say — **"I will praise the Lord."**

The desire for affection and approval often leads us down depressing paths — always seeking the love of those who reject us. Unrequited love or lack of affirmation is difficult to endure. However, when we pursue love and recognition by any means, we miss the way of faith. The Lord is our identity, not who loves us on earth. None of us will ever be loved the way Jesus loves us. He must be enough, for His love endures forever. If we are not satisfied with Him, jealousy will make us stumble. What would happen to your inner life if today, right now ... in your stressful situation, you said — "**This Time** I will praise the Lord!"

BATTLE OF THE BRIDES (GEN. 30)

Jealousy fills Rachel as she sees her sister give birth to four sons while she remains childless. With this strange triangle of domestic affairs, Rachel runs to Jacob and demands that he gives her a child. Angrily, he meets her tantrum with indignation, reminding her that only God could give a baby to her. It is good to remember that whatever we want that we do not have, it is God who withholds it! Rachel finally gives her maidservant, Bilhah to sleep with Jacob that she may provide a child for her. The child of this scheme was **Dan** ('he has vindicated,' or 'judge'). Rachel really believed that God had vindicated her action by giving her a son.

It is amazing how easily our hearts can be convinced that we are right when we lean on the flesh instead of walk in faith. It was mercy from God, not a wholesale vindication of Rachel's deeds. The second child with Jacob and Bilhah was Naphtali, meaning 'obtained by wrestling' or 'my struggle.' Rachel's statement by naming him **Naphtali** was that she had wrestled the affection of her husband out of Leah's hands by having this son. She obtained through wrestling.

Leah, refusing to be outdone, gives her maidservant, Zilpah, to Jacob — now he has 4 women in his household! The son born of Zilpah and Jacob was named, **Gad**. His name means 'good fortune' or, 'a troop comes;' indicating that Leah was going to have more children after Gad. The second child of Zilpah was a son named **Asher** — 'happy.' Leah's knew others would call her happy since she had another son. What a fascinating story of the birth of the 12 tribes of Israel (Jacob)! The saga continues....

Rachel has yet to bear a child. Leah has given birth to three sons, but the Lord has now shut her womb. They both gave their maidservants to Jacob and each gave birth to two more sons. What a household this must have been! Two sisters, each competing for the love of one man — sharing a household with two surrogate families!

Reuben, Leah's oldest son, grew weary of what was happening between his mother and his aunt. Realizing that his mother was barren again, he went out to the fields to bring a fertility herb[28] to this mother. Rachel sees Reuben returning with the mandrakes ... Fearing that Leah would become pregnant, she pleads with her sister to share the mandrakes with her. When Leah refused, Rachel struck a deal ... Rachel would allow Jacob to spend a night of intimacy with Leah, in exchange for Reuben's mandrakes!

Leah chose intimacy over the means of the flesh (mandrakes). Instead of trusting in the flesh, she cried out in faith to God, and God listened to Leah. That night she became pregnant and bore Jacob a son named Issachar — 'reward.' Issachar is a picture of **Intercession** and the reward of believing God.[29]

Leah again gives birth to a sixth son (including the two with Zilpah) and named him Zebulun, assuming that Jacob would now give honor to her. Zebulun means 'honor' or 'dwelling.' She presumed that because of the honor of giving Jacob six sons, he would now want to dwell with her instead of Rachel. Some time later, Leah gave birth to a daughter named Dinah — 'judgment.'

After seven years of barrenness, the Lord also touches Rachel as she too asked for a child. She gives birth to a son called Joseph. His name is significant in two ways. The Hebrew word *'asap'* means 'taken away' (i.e. Rachel's barrenness removed) and a similar sounding word, *'yosep,'* meaning, 'he shall add.' Joseph expressed Rachel's desire to have another son. Perhaps Leah's example of praying for a son led Rachel to also seek the Lord for a miracle child. How often in Scripture do we see God waiting until we *Ask* for the miracle?

The sad part of this story is the struggle for love and recognition between people chosen by God. To compete for one another's love is to forget the true Source of satisfaction and affirmation that is in the Lord alone. He loves us beyond measure. He calls us His delight and joy (Psalm 16:4). Whatever place we find ourselves in life — rejected or ignored, oppressed or hated, we must cultivate wholehearted trust in God and find all our joy in being loved by Him. Notice below the names of the children — and the message God wants to give us!

➤ *Reuben*: **See, a Son!** We see the Son of His love, Jesus!

➤ *Simeon*: **He who hears!** Faith comes by **hearing** of Him!

➤ *Levi*: **Joined!** When we believe we are **joined** to Him!

➤ *Judah*: **Praises!** Jesus puts praises in our hearts!

➤ *Dan*: **Judgment!** We pass **judgment** on our flesh, dying to self!

➤ *Naphtali*: **Wrestling!** We **wrestle** with the flesh, but He wins!

➤ *Gad*: **Good Fortune!** [30] The **blessings** flow as we walk with Him!

➤ *Asher*: **Happy!** What **happiness** on earth to be in love with Jesus!

➤ *Issachar*: **Reward!** The **reward** of answered prayer!

➤ *Zebulun*: **Dwelling!** Jesus is our **Dwelling** Place!

➤ *Joseph*: **He will Add!** We have **all things** in Him! God loves His Son so much; He will add others to Him as a new Man. The Father must have a family like Him!

➤ *Benjamin*: **Son of My Right Hand!** We will sit with Him for all eternity at **His Right Hand!**

Jacob is emboldened to approach Laban for permission to leave. Understanding the importance of spiritual authority, Jacob must not just pack his bags and leave. He knew Laban must first approve and release his daughters to go with Jacob. Laban does not want

them to go, for he has learned through divination that blessing has
come to his household because of the favor of God upon Jacob.
At first glance, it seems Laban's response to Jacob's request was
gracious and cordial, but Laban was selfish and wanted the blessing
on Jacob's life to make him prosperous. Perhaps this **"divination"**
was some form of witchcraft, connected to the household idols.

Jacob is quick to remind Laban he did not need an act of
divination to discover why material prosperity had visited him — it
was the blessing of the Lord. Jacob and Laban now begin to argue
over the wages Jacob is to receive. It is obvious; these two do not
trust each other! Jacob proposes a commission structure that was
somewhat tilted in Laban's favor. It was arranged in such a way that
Laban could easily determine if Jacob was cheating him.

Jacob's proposal included giving to him all of the streaked,
speckled, and spotted of Laban's flocks. From then on, Jacob's
selected breeding would insure that he was not cheating Laban. It
was a wonderful idea, but where did Jacob get it? God had appeared
to Jacob and showed him the **"streaked, speckled, spotted"** idea!
(31:10–13) He was acting on a dream from God.

Streaked, speckled, and spotted … this really describes Jacob's
soul. Full of ideas that originated in his heart, but still not broken
before God. There is much that God would do in his servant to make
him pure, untainted, and unspotted. For now, these flocks would be
a picture of where Jacob is in his walk with the God of Bethel.

God multiplied the flocks of Jacob. Blessings surround the
one whom God favors. Jacob came up with a way of breeding his
flocks that was truly unique. Perhaps from a dream or word from
God, Jacob mates the animals in front of a watering trough with
peeled branches in front of it. The animals would mate gazing
at the peeled branches — causing their offspring to come out
streaked, speckled, and spotted! This was a God-idea, shown by
the results. What appeared to be magic was really the blessing of

God. Eventually, Jacob became quite prosperous and came to own large flocks, servants, donkeys, and camels. The Lord was with this promise-bearer, the **Seed** that would bring forth the **Son** in due time. God's grace takes a man and deals with him right where he is — making him some day into a prince with God.

---

[26] Perhaps this is why the Law of Moses forbids a man to marry a woman and her sister (Lev.18:18).

[27] Leah's son Levi and his descendants become the priestly tribe of Israel.

[28] Mandrakes were recognized in this culture as a powerful fertility aid that would assist in impregnation. Also known as 'love-apples' they were fragrant and credited with limited medicinal value.

[29] (**Note:** Further study on Issachar and the type of intercession he points to, can be found in the author's book: *"Prayer Partners with Jesus"* available through *Stairway Ministries*.)

[30] Gad also means, 'a troop comes!' (i.e. many would follow after this one, an army fully prepared!) The Lord has always had a troop in His heart, and a troop comes as the image of Jesus appears within His Bride.

Chapter Fourteen

THE GOD OF BETHEL
"THE ANGEL OF GOD SAID TO ME IN A DREAM, JACOB!"

J acob had now been away from home for twenty years.
He was not to spend the remainder of his days in his uncle's household — God had a different purpose for him. Seeing the blessing of God on Jacob, Laban and his sons grew jealous. Jacob was perceived as a threat to the family inheritance. They knew that all his wealth had come from their resources.

With his in-laws not as friendly as they once were, Jacob knew it was time to go. God confirmed this to him with His word, **"Go back to the land of your fathers."** So Jacob fled from Laban with his wives and flocks, without informing Laban.

Note how God comes to Jacob with this word…. **"I am the God of Bethel, where you anointed a pillar and where you made a vow to me."** Bethel means the House of God. The 'God of the House of God' spoke to Jacob! God reminds Jacob that He is the

one who spoke to Him in the place where he turned a pillow into a
pillar! The anointed altar of devotion! Where Jacob made his vow
to serve and follow the God of Bethel! It was time to move on. The
winds of Divine purpose began to blow again. The land of promise
was calling.

Taking advantage of the three days journey that separated
Laban from him, Jacob ran off undetected. Rachel took with her
Laban's household gods. The word used here for **"gods"** is *teraphim*,
from a Syrian root word meaning, 'to inquire.'

Apparently, Laban used these images to inquire direction and
guidance by divination. Taking her father's gods would be taking
his ability to discover where they had gone (Judges 17:5, 18:6; I
Sam. 19:13; Ezek. 21:21). Other scholars believe that the teraphim
guaranteed the right of inheritance to whoever possessed them.
Rachel had become like Jacob, a deceiver.

LABAN PURSUES JACOB (31:22–42)

Laban soon found out about his family leaving. Gathering a
considerable force, Laban sets out in pursuit. On the night before
he overtook Jacob's party, God appeared to Laban in a dream and
warns him not to abuse Jacob. Clearly, God was with Jacob and was
protecting him from the anger of his father in-law.

Jacob protests his innocence to Laban in a serious dispute. All
the bottled-up bitterness in Jacob's heart comes out here. Laban
makes it clear that only the fear of God's vengeance restrains
him from use of violence. Jacob invites Laban to search their
possessions to see if they had stolen anything that belonged to
him. Obviously, he was unaware that Rachel had hidden the
family idols under the saddlebag of her camel. As Laban came
to search Rachel's stuff, she protested saying she was having her
menstrual period.

JACOB AND LABAN MAKE A COVENANT (31:43–55)

Jacob and Laban make a covenant of friendship and protection before they part company. Making a heap of stones they eat a meal of fellowship together. Laban, the Syrian, gives this heap of stones an Aramaic name. Jacob, the Hebrew, gives it a Hebrew name. In both Aramaic and Hebrew the name means, 'heap of witness.' **"It was also called Mizpah, because he said, 'May the Lord keep watch between you and me when we re away from each other.'"**

Jesus is our Mizpah. Ephesians 2:14 states that Jesus made Jew and Gentile one, breaking down the middle wall between them. Jacob a Jew and Laban a Gentile find peace at Mizpah ('watchtower'). The heap of stones was to be a witness that neither would go past these stones to harm the other. These stones would serve as boundary markers forming a treaty between the two families. All of this was made as a covenant-vow with the God of Abraham and the God of Nahor (Abraham's brother) as a Judge between them. Jacob could not swear by the God of Nahor, instead he used the phrase — "the fear of Isaac." When he deceived his father out of the blessing, Jacob showed no fear of Isaac. But after twenty years of God dealing with Jacob, he now brings a sacrifice and worships the Lord. The family of the **Spiritual Seed** makes their way toward home.

GOD'S CAMPGROUND! (GEN.32:1–21)

All along the journey home, Jacob's thoughts turned toward his offended brother Esau. Laban was behind him, but a brother who wanted to kill him was ahead. What would Esau do to him? Did he still harbor bitterness toward Jacob? How would Jacob be able to defend himself against the hostility of his brother? God was about to show the **Spiritual Seed** the spiritual protection around him....

As Jacob journeyed back to Canaan, the angels of God met him. Can you imagine what that was like? His eyes were opened to the spirit realm and the angels of heaven appeared. The angels of the Lord encamp around about those who fear Him (Ps. 34:7)! They came to welcome Jacob into his inheritance, into Canaan land (Heb. 1:14). A face-to-face encounter with two camps of angels![31] Jacob exclaimed, **"This is the camp of God!"** Jacob believed he had stumbled into the very headquarters of heaven — God's campsite!

Exactly how long Jacob interacted with the angels we do not know. He named the place **"Mahanaim"** or 'two camps.' Ancient rabbis taught that this where two camps of angels came together around Jacob. One camp from Mesopotamia that brought Jacob to the border of Canaan, and one camp of angels of Canaan that welcomed the patriarch into the land of promise. The angels danced that day as Jacob neared his destiny (Song of Songs 6:13). Encircling him they celebrated the purpose of God coming to pass with this one who returned home. The prodigal son had returned!

Mahanaim, like Bethel, was a spot where the heavenly world made contact with the earth; the invisible realm was opened to the visible. But what little effect the visitation of angels had upon Jacob! His fear of Esau returned. He knew that he had stolen a birthright and robbed his brother of the blessings of the inheritance. Perhaps this is why he sent Esau 550 animals (a tithe? 28:22). He was trying to return some of the stolen birthright!

Jacob cleverly schemed once again. He tries to *manage* Esau, instead of leaning on the Lord. Jacob sent some servants to inform **"my *master* Esau"** of what has transpired, hoping to find favor. He coaches the messengers what to tell Esau but his servants returned only to inform Jacob that Esau was still coming — with 400 men with him! **"In great fear and distress,"** he was sure he was about to be overrun with 401 men seeking vengeance. So he devises a plan. Dividing the people into two camps (borrowing the idea from the angels!); he wanted to insure that some of his stuff and family would survive. After all, half is better than none, right? This is the human heart, the 'Jacob' that lives in each of us. We always have a plan, a clever idea, something that can keep us from having to seek God. No sooner does he stop praying that he resumes the scheming!

There are times that planning will not do, we must pray. To mix planning with praying will divert us from abandonment to God's ways. Our plans will destroy our praying — our praying will destroy our planning! When we lean on God, we do not lean on our understanding. When our heart is filled with our ideas, we are still managing our lives. The Lord wants to bring us to the place where life is beyond our control; watching God work as we pray … and trust.

For some, prayer is not a voice of faith and dependence, but a voice trying to convince God of our ideas. We assume our plans must be the only way God can deliver us — but His ways are not ours. True faith is asking God to do it all. *God plus nothing = my deliverance!* So Jacob prayed. He called God, the God of his father Abraham, and God of his father, Isaac. This is God in *covenant relationship.* He was laying hold of the faithfulness of God. Then he cast himself upon the Word God had spoken — **"Go back to your country and relatives and I will prosper you."** It was a prayer of faith in the promise of God.

Acknowledging his unworthiness compared to the kindness shown him, he takes a lowly place before God and asks for Divine protection. **"I am unworthy"** is always proper when we come to God. Humility is the true friend of prayer. Jacob knew that God had provided for him everything he owned. He came to Laban with only a staff, now he leaves with great wealth. He reminds the Lord of the covenant promise of a seed, descendants which cannot be counted. Jacob prayed, and then he planned again....

He chose to bribe Esau with gifts. This is not faith at work, but a strategy to soften Esau's heart and bring reconciliation. These extravagant presents were divided into three parts, with a space between each; spreading them out to gain the best advantage. Clever. He instructed his servants what to say when they brought Esau the gifts. When asked who was sending these flocks and herds, the messengers were to simply say, **"They belong to *your servant*, Jacob. They are a gift sent to *my lord* Esau."** Jacob obviously humbles himself (or seems to) before Esau to pacify his wrath. Each group of gifts came with the message that Jacob would be coming behind. Jacob was hiding behind his bribes. A star performance!

JACOB'S ENCOUNTER WITH THE WRESTLING MAN (32:22–32)

So the flocks and herds went on ahead of him, but Jacob spent the night in the camp at Mahanaim. Afraid for his family, he sent them over the brook Jabbok with all his possessions. Jacob was alone. All alone, right where God wanted him. To be left alone with God is the only true way of coming to self-discovery. All flesh is like grass. We see ourselves as a tree, tall and upright. God calls our flesh grass, in the dirt, needing to be cut down, soon to wither. This is the turning point for Jacob. Schemes have failed, now it is he and God alone.

We can never get a true understanding of our ways until we weigh them in the balance of His presence. This is how we get a correct judgment of our selves. For God to use a man, He must first break the man and empty him of self. The name of this brook was a prophecy of what God was doing in his servant. Jabbok means *'emptying.'* We often pray, 'Lord, fill us!' But we need to ask, 'Lord, empty us!' It takes the work of God to empty our proud hearts and fill us with a nature that will be suitable for God to use.

God was taking everything away from Jacob ... his wealth, his family, now his clever confidence. Have you ever visited the brook Jabbok? More than a dream, the dark night brought One out of the shadows to deal with unbroken Jacob. The eyes of Jacob would not discern who it was coming out of the shadows, even as Jacob's father, Isaac, could not discern who it was that received his blessing. It was not Jacob wrestling a man, but a Man wrestling with Jacob. The One whom Jacob saw at the top of the stairway at Bethel had come down to wrestle with him ... to roll in the mud of his mistakes.

The Midnight Wrestling Man has come to drain Jacob of self; to wrestle from him the confidence that he could handle every situation. In the mud of Jabbok Jacob saw that he was poor, feeble, and clever in himself. When we wrestle with another, one will be overcome. One will be pinned to the ground, unable to squirm away. Can you picture puny Jacob wrestling with this Man? How silly. Yet how often do we resist the pure ways of God for our own? Up to this point, we have seen Jacob squirming out of every difficulty. Now he will meet One who is stronger than he. The one who would become an overcomer must first be overcome. The Jacob in you must be subdued for God's purpose to be fulfilled. How we must all experience this, in order to know the power of the Cross.

This Midnight Wrestling Man is Jesus Christ! He alone knows where to touch us in that place of self-confidence, the hollow of our thigh. The thigh is the strongest muscle in the human body. It is the place of our natural strength. Jacob must be broken *there*. The sinews of the old nature must be shriveled; that our new nature, whose only strength is in clinging, may come forth in power. This was the goal of that mysterious 6-hour wrestling match. The Midnight Wrestling Man will continue to 'pin' us until our love of self is shattered. We, like Jacob, must 'bite the dust' of our own nature. The Hebrew word for wrestle literally means, *'to get dusty.'* The Wrestling Man forced him to the ground, tasting the dust of the earth. This was more than an all night prayer meeting ... Jacob had to taste of his dust-nature.

Has this Man found you out? Has He come to you in recent

days to reveal your need? Has He pulled from you things long cherished and loved ... so that all you could do was to cling to Him? Have you felt as if some Mighty Power were wrestling with you for your good?

Fear not, young Jacob ... God will finish His work with you as He did with this patriarch! The Lord will meet us where we are. He will appear to us in a way that will change us. To Abraham, the pilgrim, the Lord appeared as a traveler (Gen.18). To Joshua, the general, He appeared as a soldier (Josh.5:13–15). To Jacob, one who wrestled all his life with Isaac, Esau, Laban, even his wives, the Lord came as the Midnight Wrestling Man.

Jacob did not now who this Man really was. He did not realize He was wrestling with the Covenant Man, Yahweh! Many of the restrictions and oppositions you feel in life are actually the strong arms of this Wrestling Man keeping you from having **Your** way. The Lord knows that only His ways will be peace and life to us. Our difficulties are often the 'surprise attack' of God in our inner man, showing us where we boast, where we are clever and self-sufficient. A crisis beyond our control is the only way most of us will learn to lean on Him. Eventually we discover the One who is wrestling with us is our Friend, our Redeemer!

The prolonged hand-to-hand combat lasted all night. Then, by a mere touch, Jacob's thigh went out of joint. How painful this was! Isaiah was touched on his lips, but with Jacob it must be his thigh. With muscles cramping, unable to see clearly in the dark night, Jacob wrestled an opponent much stronger than himself. Did Jacob think it was Esau that had come to him? Maybe he thought this Man was an enemy sent to harm him. Before sunrise, Jacob would discover it was the Lord of the Covenant he was struggling with.

Forget about Esau, Jacob had to deal with God! The Lord knew that it would take more than human strength to conquer Jacob (i.e. Laban,Esau).It would require a supernatural blow to his pride,his inner strength. The Lord knows how to touch the thing within us that stands against Him.

Do you know what an intense struggle is like? Have you ever 'wrestled' with God through the night over an issue you had to settle? Have you felt the pain of being 'pinned' — forced to yield, becoming a living sacrifice (Rom.12:1)? Have you felt crippled afterward? God's way of preparing His **Spiritual Seed** is to break them at the threshold of receiving their inheritance.

Jacob grabbed a heel, God grabbed his thigh! It is through these private encounters with the Lord that we become those whose names have been changed, transformed ones — subdued by the power of God (Phil. 3:21). Jacob would enter the land with a limp! Have you ever realized that when Jacob walked toward Esau and bowed down to him, he was limping? Esau would not see a whole Jacob, but a crippled Jacob. Do not be surprised when others catch you limping!

Jacob did the only thing he could. He clung to the Midnight Wrestling Man in desperation. Just as the darkness was giving way to light, Jacob held even tighter to this strange Friend. **"I will not let You go unless You bless me."** Jacob longed for the blessing and would do anything to obtain it. To wrestle with God in rebellion is foolish. But to wrestle with Him over receiving our inheritance is a mark of determination that God will bless. Is this how you take hold of the Lord? Do you pray with intensity like this? Do you refuse to let Him go until you are blessed and filled? If the blessing is worth anything, it is worth everything. We will find Him when we search (wrestle) for Him with all our hearts (Jer. 29:13).

Perceiving this was a Supernatural Man who would have the power to bless or curse, Jacob refused to release Him until a blessing was pronounced. To say this from the heart and is the secret of true strength. We borrow from One who has everything to give. Our strength is a borrowed strength. We must be weak before we can be strong. Our clever abilities will never be a pedestal on which to display the power or grace of Christ. Content in weakness, we cling to the Source of true power. So, even in our miserable situations, we may hold on to Him who has the power to make it a blessing to our soul. The entire book of Job is the Holy Spirit's commentary on this scene in Jacob's history....

"What is your name?" A strange question ... didn't God know his name? Jacob knew why God asked ... God touched not only his thigh, but also his slumbering conscience. In asking this question, Jacob's imagination took him back over 20 years in the dark tent where his blind, aged father had faced him with the same question.... *"I am Esau"* and he got away with it! That was 20 years ago ... now the Father of Eternity had come to Jacob insisting he acknowledge that he was the one who took advantage of his father and his brother.

We must all face our true nature if we want to be truly free. Jacob means heel-grabber, supplanter. The Lord was insisting that His blessings would begin when Jacob realized the true nature of his heart. By giving his name, Jacob had to confess his true nature. 'I am a deceiver, a cheat. My name is Sinner.' This confession liberated Jacob, opening the way for inner transformation. Jacob was forgiven.

"Your name will no longer be Jacob, but Israel." Only the Lord has the authority and power to transform us. Jacob was face to face with the God of Abraham and his father Isaac. He encountered in the gleams of the sunrise, the Light of Israel. His outward limp spoke of God's inward victory — the victorious limp of God's prince, God's Israel. (Israel means 'prince with God' or 'reigning with God') Jacob held tight until the blessing came. For this, his name was changed. This is how true transformation takes place:

➢ God initiates change by orchestrating life to expose our weakness.

➤ We will be led to a place where clever schemes cannot deliver.

➤ When it looks the worst, out of the shadows comes our Foe/Friend.

➤ He will force us to look at our own nature and bite the dust!

➤ He will 'pin us to the mat' until we cry 'uncle' (or is it 'Father')!

➤ We acknowledge that our nature is to depend on self, not God.

➤ God will touch us and cripple our pride.

➤ As we are crushed, He changes our heart; giving us a new identity.

Jacob wanted to know the name of the One who conquered him....
"Please tell me your name...." **"Why do you ask me my name"** was
the response. We need not ask His name. Through Jacob's experience
we can learn the name of the One who wrestles with us. For one, the
Lord's name may be *'husband.'* For another, the Lord's name may
be *'wife.'* For yet another, the name of the Lord may be *'unyielding
spiritual leader'* or *'obnoxious coworker.'* Our Redeemer will come
with different faces to subdue our unbroken hearts.

Our real problem is never another person; it is always our
natural strength. Most believers devote their attention to dealing
with outward sin, shortcomings, and worldliness of some sort
— never thinking that their natural strength is what the Lord
must touch. He is not only concerned with our outward life, but
with our inward, natural life. True transformation is the internal
touch at the place of our greatest confidence, where we lean
on our own wisdom and abilities. Those areas within where we
can live without His grace will all be touched before the Lord is
finished with us.

Although the Lord did not reveal His name, He did impart a
blessing. The blessing of perpetual weakness, the blessing of knowing
our heart. Jesus taught that knowing truth sets the soul free. When
we can admit our need, realizing the truth of our 'dust' life, we are
the one who is truly free. Free from pretending, free from the 'camera

pose.' Jacob named that place, **Peniel** — 'the face of God.'

How little do we understand that the Lord's wrestling with us through the dark night reveals His face...? Jacob saw the face of Love. Face to Face — Jacob and the Creator God! The face of God is the Light of God that exposed the need of Jacob. His light will give us a mortal blow. Once we are enlightened, we realize that our boasts — what we considered good, outstanding — are vain and foolish. Jacob survived that midnight encounter. As the sun rose upon him, he received the revelation of a new day! Now that he had seen God face to face, he could look Esau directly in the eye....

"Jacob looked up and there was Esau, coming with his four hundred men." Genesis 33:1

---

[31] This angelic welcoming committee had actually been with Jacob all the time. They were the ones blessing, guarding, and guiding Jacob through life.

Chapter Fifteen

BROTHERS UNITED
"THERE WAS ESAU, COMING WITH HIS
FOUR HUNDRED MEN."

Esau comes with 400 men; Jacob comes with 4 women and his children. Jacob divides his children by their mothers, and sends them to Esau one group at a time. The most loved of all to Jacob were Rachel and Joseph, those he reserved for last, just in case the anger of Esau breaks out against him and his family. Jacob is a clever, thoughtful man — but he is still walking in the wisdom of man. He anticipated vengeance from the hand of Esau, so he exposes those he cared about the least to the first stroke of that vengeance. The 400 men were merely attendants of Esau, not an army to wipe him out!

Jacob approaches Esau, bowing seven times — a little 'overkill' to insure his gesture of friendship with his estranged brother. Remember, Jacob comes limping to Esau.... The younger bowed down before the elder. This is the way to recover peace where it has been broken — respect for others will always win you favor. The word of the Midnight Wrestling Man was true — Israel would prevail with others. Esau embraced Jacob and they wept together....

How pleasant to be restored to a brother! Imagine the sense of emotional release Jacob (Israel) felt as he stood there hugging Esau. It is good to remember that in a moment, God can turn enemies into friends. Remember that God turned Saul into Paul! Our hearts must always be postured to reconcile with others who have distanced themselves from us.

As Jacob and Esau wept in each other's arms, the women and children began to appear. First the handmaidens with their children, then Leah with her children, then at last, Rachel and Joseph (his favoritism apparent). Esau was stunned, moved in his heart as he discovered how God had blessed his brother with such a family. The oldest would only be 14, the youngest, a mere infant. How touching! Uncle Esau was moved deeply....

Jacob speaks of his children as gifts from God. How we wish every dad would see their children that way and fulfill their God-given role of loving and nurturing their young. Jacob's wives and children all pass before Uncle Esau. He refused the gifts sent to him because he too, was a man of means and had sufficient supply. Esau did not need it for he was rich, nor did he need it to be pacified — he was reconciled with his brother.

Jacob again prevails ... He pleads with Esau to take the gifts. Remarkably, Jacob tells Esau that being reconciled to him is like seeing the face of God. Jacob saw God's favor (face) in the mending of this relationship. How sweet is forgiveness, how pleasant to the soul when we are made one again with those we love! It is like gazing on the face of God. We see God most clearly when we touch mercy and forgiveness.

Are there some in your life that need to see the face of God in your countenance? Could you show them a side of God they perhaps have never seen … forgiveness … even if they were wrong? Every time we encounter an offended brother we see the face of God. If we have sinned, when we see that one whom we have offended, we will see God if the matter is not settled. Every time we see their face, we will be reminded of God.…

JACOB WORSHIPS (33:16–20)

Jacob made it seem like he would catch up with Esau at Seir, but he did not. He left for another place — Succoth ('booths' or 'shelters'). Succoth was in the opposite direction of Seir where Jacob had told Esau he was coming. Perhaps Jacob was not anxious to see the face of his father, whom he had deceived.

In Succoth Jacob built shelters for himself and his livestock, but no mention of building the house of the Lord — Jacob built no altar at Succoth. The wanderer now begins to settle down — but only for a while. God's plans for Jacob would not be fulfilled here; he must venture forward. We are too quick to build a shelter for ourselves, only to discover there is more waiting ahead.

"After Jacob came from Paddan Aram, he arrived safely ('at Shalem') **at the city of Shechem in Canaan and camped within sight of the city."** The word "safely" can also mean peace or a place called Shalem (Salem). Shechem means 'shoulder' — the place of strength. Jacob at last enters Canaan and camps near the ancient site of Jerusalem! Interestingly, this is the first place his grandfather Abram, camps as he entered the Promised Land. Abraham set out to look for that city, Jacob now camps within sight of it. The work of God has advanced … the **Spiritual Seed** is moving toward the Eternal City!

"For a hundred pieces of silver, he bought from the sons of Hamor, the father of Shechem, the plot of ground where he pitched his tent." Jacob saw a treasure in that place of anointing, Shalem. Finding a treasure in the field, he bought the field with a hundredfold obedience (100 pieces of silver). Although it was his by the promise of God, he paid the price to own the field. Throughout the Bible, we will see it is those who pay the full price of obedience to God that inherit the blessing.

We learn from the story found in John 4 of the woman of Samaria, that there was a in the vicinity of Sychar (Shechem) a piece of land which was bought by Jacob and given to his son, Joseph (John 4:5, Josh.24:32). The well spoken of in John 4 was Jacob's well. Jesus sat on top of the very place where Jacob dwelt at Shechem. Jacob had no clue that His **Seed** would indeed sit upon that well someday. The long awaited Messiah patiently won the soul of a sinful woman at Shechem. The Mighty God of Israel visited the well of Shechem!

"There he set up an altar and called it El Elohe Israel." At Shechem, the place of strength, Jacob builds an altar to the Lord — calling it 'Mighty is the God of Israel!' He glorifies the Lord for the change of his name to Israel. Now He will be the God of Israel. He dedicates this altar to God, the God of Israel or Mighty is the God of Israel. Perhaps the altar erected by his grandfather had fallen down — Jacob merely rebuilding it. But it is hard to worship God in a place we are not meant to be....

Regardless, this was a milestone in the life of the patriarch. Jacob had now arrived in the land ... But Jacob must still go further ... he must return to Bethel and finish building the House of the Lord. God had already revealed Himself as the God of Bethel ... this is where Jacob must go to find Him fully!

DINAH DEFILED (34:1–31)

After Jacob had settled in Shechem, Leah's daughter, Dinah went out to visit the women of the land. She went to not only see the women of the land, but to be seen by them as well. Perhaps they introduced her to Shechem, the ruler of the city that was named after him. Dinah was likely 15 or 16 years old at this time. The Scriptures record that Shechem *"violated her."*[32] Shechem fell in love with Jacob's daughter and sent his father, Hamor to arrange a marriage.

"Jacob heard that ... Dinah had been defiled." At the very time Hamor was speaking with Jacob, the sons of Jacob returned from the fields and learned of the sexual violation of their sister. **"They were filled with grief and fury."** quite a description of their feeling toward Shechem.

Hamor pleads with them to allow the marriage, for his son, Shechem is truly in love with Dinah. He encourages them to form a treaty, giving them freedom to interact, intermarry, and trade with the people of the land. Jacob's sons, filled with the thought of revenge, deceitfully gave consent with one condition — all the men of the land must be circumcised. The reason for this would be obvious ... they would be incapacitated and unable to resist when they fell upon them. Never suspecting a problem, they submitted to the surgery.

With the men in pain, Levi and Simeon took their swords and killed the men of the city. Removing Dinah from the house of Shechem, they took all the wealth of the city to themselves. The deception, brutal murder and ransacking of the city was wrong and brought great disgrace to Jacob. Jacob expresses his fear that retribution would come from the Canaanites and Perizzites remaining in the land. Once again, Jacob feared for his life because of offending others.

BACK TO BETHEL (35:1–9)

God's purpose for Jacob was to lead him to Bethel, the House of God. It is only at the 'House of God' that we understand our destiny (Ps.27:4). Jacob vowed to return and build the House of the Lord at Bethel. It was time for Jacob to pay his vow and touch the Anointed Stone. God speaks a word that brings conviction and revival to Jacob, **"Go up to Bethel and settle there."**

It was at Bethel thirty years ago that he met the Lord and gazed into the heavens, seeing the Jesus Stairway. First-love devotion will be restored as we make the move to Bethel....

What is it about Bethel that is so important? God is looking for a habitation, a dwelling place. The Bible begins with Creation but ends with Habitation. Progressively, the Creator is preparing to dwell with man. Bethel is the House of God, His dwelling place. After Bethel, there was the Tabernacle in the wilderness; after that was the Temple of Solomon ... and in time, God dwelt with man in **Man**, Jesus Christ (Isa.7:14, John 1:14). Now the Church is the Dwelling Place of God, His Living Room (I Cor.3:16, Eph.2:19–22). Bethel is the beginning; the New Jerusalem will be the culmination. Jacob must take the steps of building an altar and dedicating the House of God.

"God ... answered me in the day of my distress." This was a true revival for Jacob. He calls for a time of cleansing for everyone in his household. The first thing they had to do was to remove the idols, those that Rachel took years ago when they fled from Laban. When the Lord refreshes His people we have the desire to 'clean house' and remove the unclean things from our lives. Some of the acceptable 'idols' in the church today would include: your education, your ambition even in the church, ministry can be an idol that some leaders cannot let go of, your desires can replace God, your friends or children, or spouse may all become idols. Building an altar must be more important than building a future.

The second thing he tells them is **"purify yourselves."** They needed to bathe themselves in the purity of God. Cleansing the heart is a constant need for all that want endless revival. Every pollution of the soul must be removed (II Cor.7:1). **Then** Jacob tells them to 'change your clothes' — a new beginning, a fresh start!

Our old clothes speak of our old life that must be laid aside as we put on Christ (Is.64:6, Rev.3:18). Changing our garments is to change our manner of life and put on a new man. All the people obeyed Jacob, forsaking their idols. To fully bury their past, Jacob buried the idols under the oak at Shechem. Perhaps the **"rings in their ears"** were idols which needed to be abandoned (Hos.2:13). Altar-builders must be cleansed from secret sins.

What was the result of this revival in Jacob's house? As they set out for Bethel, **"the terror of God fell upon the towns all around them so that no one pursued them."** After the idols were removed, hearts were cleansed, and new garments placed upon Jacob and his household. The terror of God falls on entire towns! If God be for us, who could be against us? This was a powerful anointing released as sins were confessed and forsaken. Nothing terrifies the enemy like the purification of the saints. Instead of fighting the enemy we can see them terrified by our clean hearts! Its time to terrify your enemies!

Upon arriving at Bethel, Jacob builds an altar and offers sacrifice to God. He names the altar, **"El Bethel," which means** 'God of Bethel,' or 'The God of the House of God.' This is a major turning point in the life of Jacob. He is where he belongs, surrendering his life and future into the hands of El Bethel. He is lost in the purposes of God. Before this, God was called the God of a certain person — for example, the God of Abraham or the God of Isaac. However, in 35:7, He is the God of the House of God. He is no longer the God of individual persons; He is now the God of a corporate body, the House of God.

The New Testament counterpart to Bethel is the church (ITim.3:15). For us, Bethel is not history; it is the church of the Living God. We are not just a pile of individual stones; we are being built into the House of God. We must all experience Him in such a way that He becomes more to us than just our individual God, but the God of the House of God. This is why we come together as a body — to find the God of the House of God. It is time to come to El Bethel.

There is a puzzling statement made in verse 8, **"Deborah, Rebekah's nurse, died and was buried under the oak below Bethel. So it was named Allon Bacuth."** There are no wasted words in the Bible. Since Deborah was Rebekah's nurse, she likely was very close to Jacob after his mother, died. Deborah was a great comfort to Jacob in the loss of his mother, but now, she too is taken from him. At the very time he surrenders to God at Bethel, his main source of comfort was removed, forcing Jacob to lean upon his Source and Encouragement.

The day will come when God will take away your 'nursing mothers' and bring you into a deeper confidence in Him. We often turn to our friends and loved ones to sympathize with us, to soothe and comfort our weary hearts. In due time, our 'Deborah' will be removed that the God of Bethel will be **All** to us. We do not need sympathy or nursing, we really need **Him**!

In this passage we see that three things were buried — the idols, the earrings, and Deborah. They were all buried under an oak tree — a symbol of flourishing life. Notice all these things must be buried **Below** Bethel. The House of God must be on the highest plane, everything placed beneath His feet. This burial oak was named Allon Bacuth — The Oak of Weeping. It is always painful to the flesh to give up and surrender all to God. May the Lord bring us to the Oak of weeping where all is abandoned to Him.

ISRAEL (GEN.35:10–15)

"After Jacob returned from Paddan Aram, God appeared to him again and blessed him." The result of this total yielding to God and burying his past brought a new revelation of God to Israel. The Lord appears and confirmed the change of his name to Israel and gives Jacob the revelation of His Name — El Shaddai, **"God Almighty."** Every time we yield our heart to Jesus and give Him more of our affections, we will encounter Him in a new way.

"God said to him, 'Your name is Jacob, but you will no longer be called Jacob; your name will be Israel.' So he named him Israel." God seemed to be saying — *'Did I not change your name to Israel? Why do you keep calling yourself Jacob? Do not call yourself Jacob, for that means you will live and behave yourself as you have in the past. This is a new day for you. You must show yourself as an overcomer, a prince. See yourself as Israel and live by the light of what I have done!'* God doesn't want to multiply Jacob, but Israel.

"And God said to him, "I am God Almighty; be fruitful and increase in number." Life comes from God Almighty. Because He is all-powerful fruit and life can spring up from you and me. The command to be fruitful and multiply is rooted in God's power to make it happen. His Almightiness is available to you! You can be fruitful in your walk with Him and multiply yourself into many new believers because El-Shaddai is with you. If you will trust Him as God Almighty your life will bear genuine fruit to His glory.

"A nation and a community of nations will come from you, and kings will come from your body. The land I gave to Abraham and Isaac I also give to you, and I will give this land to your descendants after you." Kings will come forth from this limping man who has prevailed with God. The kings point to the kingdom — not only the kingdom of David and Solomon, but also the kingdom of God. The land is divinely deeded to Israel and his descendants.

These words to Jacob are a reaffirmation and continuation of God's promise to Abraham, Jacob's grandfather. We see four things that are identical to the promises given to Abraham in Gen.17:4–6.

➤ A name change (Abram to Abraham – Jacob to Israel).

➤ A promise that kings will come from them.

➤ A reference to being fruitful.

➤ A promise that a multitude of nations will come from them.

The promise of a multitude (Lit. 'congregation') of nations will come from the **Spiritual Seed**. Paul states that Abraham is "the father of us all" (Rom.4:16–17). Abraham and Jacob did not seem to become a father of many nations in the physical sense. So Paul is presenting the possibility that this fruitfulness and multiplication includes spiritual children, not just physical descendants. Everyone has a claim to this promise as they come in faith to the incarnation of the **Spiritual Seed**, Jesus Christ (Gal.3:16). Faith, not Jewishness makes you a child of Abraham, the father of all who *believe.*[33]

"Then God went up from him at the place where He had talked with him." This was not an angel. It was the very glory cloud of His presence! In chapter 28, Jacob had a dream. But now it was not a dream, but a Divine Encounter. The Hebrews teach that God appeared to Jacob out of the Shekinah glory cloud that came down upon the altar built for God. Jacob again sets up a stone pillar at Bethel and pours out a "drink offering" upon the altar, along with oil. Oil and Wine were poured out at Bethel! See Ex.29:40–41, Num.6:17, 15:1–5, 28:7–10, II Sam.23:16. This brings Jacob to the very place of fellowship restored with God. The pillar becomes a picture of the overcoming life (Rev.3:12).

Jacob himself is the drink offering that is poured out to God. The drink offering was a unique offering that was offered by a priest in gratitude for the first fruits of harvest (Lev.23:10–13). Often, it was poured out upon another offering. As Paul was about to be martyred, he was *"poured out like a drink offering on the sacrifice and service"* of the faith of his friends (Phil2:17, II Tim.4:6). When Paul said he was being poured out like a drink offering, he meant he was willing to yield all his life and joy (wine) to the excellency of Christ; even if it cost his life. If we could talk with the martyrs, they would tell us that their martyrdom was just a pouring out upon the sacrifice of Christ the joy of their whole being. They experienced Christ so much; they themselves were poured out as a drink offering upon the sacrifice Jesus made for them. Are you willing to give it all up and be poured out in the Lord's presence?

God enjoys drinking wine. He does not seek the wine made from grapes, but the wine made from Christ saturating the soul of the passionate lover of God (Song of Songs 4:10). Your spirit can become the wine of God as He fills you with heavenly joy and abandon. Becoming His satisfaction, you will be poured out before Him until **He** becomes all there is. As we pour out the wine, Jesus pours out the oil of the Spirit. The more we are prepared to be poured out as a drink offering, the more of the oil we will enjoy. This is the Anointed Pillar of the House of God. Oil and Wine — the abandonment of man to God, and God to man....

RACHEL'S DEATH & BENJAMIN'S BIRTH (35:16–22)

As important as Bethel was to Jacob, still he must move on. As they were traveling, Rachel went into labor. With great difficulty in childbirth, Rachel died. As she breathed her last, she named the son Ben-Oni (son of my sorrow). "But his father named him Benjamin" (son of my right hand). Her labor pains gave birth to Benjamin, but caused her death. She once passionately said to her husband — "Give me children or else I die" — and now that she had her children, she died. By naming him, 'son of my sorrow' she left a legacy for him that Israel was not comfortable with. He changed his name to 'son of my right hand' — Benjamin, an act of faith and hope for Jacob.

Rachel's weeping was also for those sons who would be killed by Herod 1,700 years later (Matt.2:16–18). Her tears were a prophecy of what was coming to her sons (the Benjaminites settled near Bethlehem!). In the entire universe there is only one **Son** that is both *Son of Sorrow* and *Son of the Right Hand*! Jesus is His Name! Christ is a Wonderful Person with these two aspects to His Name. Isaiah 53:3 describes Him as the "Man of Sorrows" while Acts 2:33

tells us that He has been "exalted to the right hand of God." Mary, the mother of Jesus also experienced pain. The prophet spoke over her, *"a sword will pierce your own soul too (Luke 2:35)."* When her Son was raised from the dead, He rose to be the Son of God's right hand. There is no doubt that Benjamin was a type of the suffering and exalted Christ!

Jacob buried his beloved Rachel near to the place where she died. So soon after his Divine Encounter at Bethel did sorrow fill his heart. Great afflictions can follow great joys. Jacob sets up a pillar[34] over the tomb of Rachel at Bethlehem (I Sam.10:2) which Moses states that "to this day that pillar marks Rachel's tomb." While this may mean little to us, it mean so much to the Israelites as they came into the Promised Land centuries later under Joshua's leadership and see standing Jacob's pillar. What a sense of history this pillar gives!

When you pour yourself out as a drink offering, God will take you serious. You will have no choice. If God takes the dearest thing to you, bless His Name. The way of Rachel, is the way of every disciple. We labor to give forth the life of Christ, but must die before He will be seen in us. Sorrow leads to exaltation when we are willing to die to bring Him forth. It will always require hard labor to bring forth Christ in His people (Gal.4:19).

All of this happened close to Ephrath, which means 'fruitful.' On the way to fruitfulness, God truly changes His servant Jacob. He was a man transformed by the visitation of God and the pain of sorrow. **Israel** journeyed forward from this day on. Jacob is called Israel.... God's deep work had been accomplished in the 'heel-holder.' Rachel dies, but Israel journeys on. Many, many years later ... *a son of Benjamin* named Paul the apostle, would lead many into the ways of Christ (Phil.3:5).

Jacob pitched his tent beyond Migdal Eder ('the watchtower of the flock') and dwelt there. Instead of pressing on to Hebron, he settled short of his destination. As he was enjoying his life, something dreadful happened. Israel's firstborn son, Reuben, slept with his father's concubine (I Cor.5:1).

Reuben's sin was more than just a satisfying of a lustful appetite.... In the culture of the day, for a son to take a father's wife was a declaration of headship of the family. Rebellious Absalom declared himself ruler by taking his father's concubines (II Sam.16:20–23). It was Reuben's purpose to usurp the headship of the family, which made his sin even more despicable.

Reuben, like the prodigal son, could not wait for his inheritance — he wanted it now. Reuben was reckless, lacking self-control. Nothing will thwart God's purpose in our life like carelessness. Although Jacob did nothing immediately, he later exposed Reuben's sin and stripped him of the rights of the firstborn, giving them to Joseph, *the firstborn with Rachel* (Gen.48:1–14, 49:3–4, I Chron.5:1–2). Later, when Joseph was tempted to adultery, he fled!

THE DEATH OF ISAAC AT HEBRON (35:23–29)

Now that Benjamin is born, we have a complete list of the children of Israel — the 12 sons and future tribes of Israel (35:23–26). Poor Leah, if only she could have known that the days would come when the two greatest offices of Israel, priest and king, would be filled by the descendants of her two sons, Levi and Judah! Aaron was a son of Levi and David was a son of Judah. Even more than that, the Messiah, Christ Jesus, was born of Judah the son of Leah!

Jacob, at last, comes to Hebron. This is the home of his father Isaac, where his grandfather Abraham once dwelt. The age and death of Isaac are recorded, and by calculation, Isaac died years after Joseph was sold into Egypt. Isaac lived the longest of all the patriarchs, 180 years (Abraham lived to 175). The death of their father brought Esau and Jacob together to mourn their loss.

Isaac's death brought great wealth and blessing to Jacob. As the head of the family and heir of the covenant blessings, Jacob was indeed full. He was about 120 years old when Isaac died. Jacob enters full fellowship with God at Hebron ('fellowship').

In this place of fellowship, we will enjoy peace, satisfaction, intimacy with God and others. Each of us must pass through Shechem (strength), Bethel (the House of God), and Hebron (fellowship). Hebron is the place of maturity and fullness. At Hebron, Jacob entered into full rest — God took away his father and freed him completely from every earthly tie.... Jacob is free at last to enjoy God in the place of sweet fellowship with his Friend.

---

[32] This violation was not necessarily rape, but could be that he convinced her to sleep with him.

[33] Galatians 3:29 & Luke 3:8

[34] Jacob built two pillars in this chapter, one to his joy and one to his sorrow.

CONCLUSION

God made a ladder and He built it for you. It stretches from the earth to the heavens. Hand-crafted by Almighty and Son — this Stairway is completed. All the work has been done. All we must do is choose climb up and look into the eyes of the King of Glory. In them we will see His divine perspective. Do you want to see what He sees? In the midst of turmoil you can see His heavenly outlook. He did not see Abram as a man with a wife who was too old to even have one child. He sees a way to show His glory to all people by doing the impossible. When we see "it's too late" — he sees opportunity. Set your eyes on the One who made Abraham a father of many nations. The God who does what He says He will do. In the middle of your desert with nothing left, lay your head on The Rock and close your eyes. The sands fade away, and a ladder appears with angels ascending and descending upon it. It is time to live in revelation of The Stairway.

Fixing our eyes on Him is how we abandon our trust to God. In seeking His ways we become living altars. In completely offering up our lives to him we declare that we keep nothing for ourselves and all is given to Him. In seeking His ways we become living altars. We are all like the altars that Abram erected throughout his desert journeys. It is only for God that we are on the earth. He is our life, and all that we are must be consumed by Him. We admit with our lives that His ways our higher than our ways.

In the end, the stairway becomes more than a supernatural experience Jacob had fleeing from his brother Esau. It stands for all time as a sign and a wonder inviting the people of God toward their heavenly calling in Christ Jesus. God longed for more than just a man. He longed for more than one nation of peoples. He longed to see every nation, tribe and tongue drawn to Himself. He loved Jesus so much that He wanted to fill Heaven with people just like Him. So he called Abram out of the land of Ur and Abram chose to seek after a city whose builder and Maker is God. When He calls us out and we choose Him we choose the Stairway. We choose to believe that even though we walk the earth we are seated in heavenly places. It is the desperate walk of the hungry to move out of our own reality and move into His. You are called to be a look-alike of Jesus. Though made from dust, we are destined for glory.

THE EDOMITES
"THIS WAS ESAU ...
THE FATHER OF THE EDOMITES"

Esau is also called Edom. The Edomites, descendants of Esau, settled near Mt. Seir (Deut.2:5, Gen.35:8). Esau had three wives with numerous children and grandchildren. His descendants are listed to the third and fourth generation, after which they are lost in obscurity. It is the line of Jacob that is the way of the Promised Seed.

The Edomites are a spiritual picture of the fleshly church; believers who are carnal and live only for the world. The church of Esau (Edom) lives by natural wisdom and cleverness instead of living moment by moment in fellowship with the Holy Spirit. Just as Esau sold his birthright to his brother Jacob for a bowl of bean soup and bread, so the Esau church today is controlled by a worldly spirit of instant gratification — with no true heart for the things of the Spirit (Rom.8:7–8). In the last days the Lord will stretch His plumb line over Edom and judge the false church (Isa. 34:11, 60:2, Jer. 13:16, Joel 2:1–2, Rev. 17:6).

In verses 20–30 there is mention of the Horites. For thousands of years there was never any evidence that the Horites even existed. It is now discovered that they were a large group of people (the Hurrians) who settled in northern Mesopotamia and in the Palestine before 2000 BC. Thousands of tablets containing their business documents and other records have been unearthed by excavation.

Throughout the history of Israel, the Edomites became enemies to God's people — a continual thorn in their side (Heb. 12: 16–17). The ancient animosity between Esau and Jacob still runs deep.

ABOUT THE AUTHOR

Dr. Brian Simmons and his wife Candice were called by God to New England while missionaries in the jungles of Central and South America. For seven years they served as church planting missionaries among the tribes. As linguists and translators, they assisted in translating the New Testament into the Kuna language.

Brian now serves as Senior Pastor of Gateway Christian Fellowship in West Haven, Connecticut. With a clear prophetic gift, signs and wonders have accompanied their ministry for many years. He travels nationally and internationally laying apostolic groundwork to see God unite the church in passion toward the Son of God, and transform her so that she may reveal Jesus Christ as the Bridegroom-King.

Brian currently serves as a member of Harvest International Ministries Apostolic Team under Dr. Ché Ahn and is a member of the International Coalition of Apostles led by Dr. C. Peter Wagner. He has spear-headed The Call New England and is the founder and president of Gateway Ministry Fellowship—a network of churches, missionaries and ministries. Under Brian's leadership, The Call School New England has been established to train and release young men and women for end-time ministry. Brian and Candice long to see this emerging generation rise to leadership and partnership for revival among the nations. Brian has authored several books including, Song of Songs: *The Journey of the Bride*, *Prayer Partners with Jesus*, *Genesis* and *Davidic Worship*. Brian and Candice have 3 children and 4 grandchildren.

THE INSPIRED ALLEGORY OF
DIVINE ROMANCE BETWEEN CHRIST
AND HIS BRIDE, THE CHURCH.

To some, the Song of Songs is a simple love story of a man and a maiden, but for those with enlightened hearts, it becomes the key that unlocks the treasure chest of Divine Love. No other portion of Scripture has such power to reveal the Sacred Journey like the Song of Songs! It is the way of a Man with a maiden ... the way our heavenly Bridegroom, Jesus Christ, transforms the heart with perfect love. The Shulamite's story is your story. For every Christian yearning to run after Jesus, this book gives you wind to fly and a map to know how to get there! *Song of Songs: Journey of the Bride* can be considered a guide to Solomon's great prophetic epic that Jesus Himself sings over you. There is One who calls you lovely even while in darkness and insecurity ... listen to this Divine Song of everlasting love given for the Princess Bride — fit for a king. You will never be the same again!

AS THE DEER PANTS FOR STREAMS OF WATER, SO MY SOUL PANTS FOR YOU, O GOD. PS. 42:1

In *Prayer Partners with Jesus*, Brian Simmons explores the many aspects of prayer, and persuades us that it is for everyone. We all begin our journey by walking toward Him, asking Him to answer our needs, and fulfill our desires. The more we walk this road the closer we get to Him, and a thirst for His Presence takes hold of our lives. In time we are no longer walking towards God, but we are walking *with* Him. Our own desires have changed as we have pursued Him, and we find ourselfves echoing the prayers of His heart. We have been transformed into an instrument that He can use to establish his plans on the earth. Since the beginning, He has been waiting on us. Yes, Heaven is waiting on earth. God is looking for a partner who will agree with Him to see His Kingdom established. We are on Heaven's Highway and *Prayer Partners with Jesus* depicts the way!

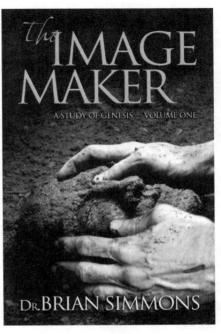

ORDER FORM

➤ ORDER ONLINE: http://www.stairwayministries.org

➤ CALL TOLL-FREE (U.S. AND CANADA): 1-877-527-0880

➤ FAX ORDERS (U.S. AND CANADA): 1-203-937-6822

➤ POSTAL ORDERS: Stairway Ministries, 129 Bull Hill Lane,
West Haven, CT 06516 USA

QUANTITY	TITLE	PRICE	TOTAL
_____	SONG OF SONGS: THE JOURNEY OF THE BRIDE	$12.00	_____
_____	PRAYER PARTNERS WITH JESUS	$12.00	_____
_____	IMAGE MAKER	$12.00	_____
_____	The Stairway	$12.00	_____
_____			_____
		SUBTOTAL	_____
	SHIPPING (20% OF SUBTOTAL)		_____
	TOTAL THIS ORDER		_____

(PLEASE PRINT CLEARLY)

NAME:_____

STREET ADDRESS: _____

APT._____ CITY:_____

STATE: _____ ZIP:_____

COUNTRY: _____ PHONE: _____

E-MAIL:_____

METHOD OF PAYMENT:

___ Check or Money Order (Make check payable to Stairway Ministries)

___ Credit Card: ___ Visa ___ MasterCard ___ American Express ___ Discover

CARD NUMBER: _____-_____-_____-_____   EXPIRATION DATE: _____/_____

Card Validation Number (last three digits on the back of your card) _____

CARD HOLDER (please print): _____

SIGNATURE:_____
(Credit card orders cannot be processed without signature)

For current shipping and handling information, call 1-877-527-0880.
Or visit our website at www.stairwayministries.org.